SO CHIC

Copyright © 2007 Filipacchi Publishing USA, Inc.
First published in the United States of America by Filipacchi Publishing
1633 Broadway, New York, NY 10019

Edited by Margaret Russell
Art direction by Florentino Pamintuan
Editorial production by Dara Keithley
Art production by Meredith McBride

ISBN: 1-933231-27-0

Printed in China

SO CHIC

GLAMOROUS LIVES, STYLISH SPACES

BY MARGARET RUSSELL

AND THE EDITORS OF

CONTENTS

DELPHINE & REED KRAKOFF

Delphine and Reed Krakoff are among the design world's most directional and in-demand tastemakers. He's the president and executive creative director of Coach, the trendsetting leather-goods company, as well as a decorative-arts connoisseur and a fervent photographer. The French-born missus is a decorator with a notably confident sense of style. So where better to observe their ardor for gorgeous objets than Southampton, where they took a 1970s modernist house and remodeled it into something where serious glamour meets mirthful chic.

All of this poses the burningly obvious question: How do two such independent-minded folks negotiate the pitfalls inherent in collaboration? Simple, says Reed, "We don't buy it unless we both like it." Significantly absent, and mercifully so, from this compact and expertly renovated retreat are the usual signifiers of contemporary hipness, those arty provocateurs who provide a shortcut to fabulousness for so many young and monied collectors. In their place, the Krakoffs have amassed the work of artists who have won the couple's loyalty because their unquenchable creativity extends beyond the confines of a gallery into the popular mediums of the day.

A quick spin through the Krakoff home reveals dose after dose of the unexpected. In one spot are graphic drawings by Jean Cocteau; in another, an impressive portrait of a soldier by Christian Bérard. Almost every room has its complement of hand-painted furniture by the illustrator Pierre Le-Tan. And in the living room stands a flock of wooly, life-size sheep that graze on a verdant David Hicks carpet. Produced in 1965 by the artist-illustrator François-Xavier Lalanne, the surreal ewes were adored by Yves Saint Laurent and Coco Chanel. As is their wont with the living designers whose work they collect, the Krakoffs have become friendly with Lalanne and his wife, Claude (they own two of her sculptures), and recently produced a book project together.

The couple's passion for provenance extends into the garden, now a showcase for sculptures by Tony Smith and Jean Arp, and even into the rooms of the couple's children, where creations by Fornasetti and Jansen hold sway. Yet the Krakoffs are no slouches on the pop culture front. An erudite discussion of a Karl Springer python-skin cocktail table can veer spontaneously into a comparison of reality-television shows. So lively are the conversations that visitors get the distinct impression that once the door closes, the Krakoffs rush back to watch another TiVo'd episode of *America's Next Top Model*—with the ghosts of Cocteau and Bérard chuckling right along. ■

INSIDE INFORMATION

▪ Collect what you love, follow your instincts, and have confidence. Don't purchase something simply because it's a good deal or what you think you should be collecting. Investing in furniture isn't like buying stocks; at the end of the day, you have to live with it.

▪ Educate yourself. Reference books are a terrific tool, but they tend to be academic; they're not about acquiring. Browse the websites of the top auction houses, attend sale previews, study catalogues. For instance, if English furniture interests you, you'll learn to see the difference between a $5,000 Queen Anne chair and one that sells for $50,000.

▪ Every period of design has great things, and my wife, Delphine, and I collect every period. But she is far more objective and pragmatic; I can be too easily influenced by the provenance of a piece. All that matters is that we like something and can mix it in with what we already own. Plus, design is cyclical—truly everything is back in style at some point.

▪ Nothing is more boring than curated rooms. The interiors that are chic and exciting are those with a confident collection of pieces that don't necessarily go together, but work well because their owner loves them. There's no better rule than that.

PRECEDING PAGES
Reed Krakoff, president and executive creative director of Coach, photographed the Southampton home he shares with his wife, Delphine, and their children for ELLE DECOR.

ABOVE
The couple flanks a vintage Saarinen Tulip table with Louis XV dining chairs upholstered in a custom-made ostrich leather from Coach; the plaster chandelier is by Olivier Gagnère.

RIGHT
The original pool and 1970s poolhouse were updated.

OPPOSITE
The sofa was custom made by Delphine Krakoff's interior design firm, Pamplemousse; the cocktail table is by Garouste and Bonetti, and the rug was made-to-order by David Hicks Paris.

LEFT
The poolhouse is furnished
with a custom-made
canvas-and-pearwood bench by Hermès, a
1950s sofa, and Tord Boontje's
Blossom chandelier
for Swarovski; the 1930s Serge Roche
plaster torchères
were purchased at auction.

LEFT
In the master bedroom, the bed is dressed
with Leontine Linens and a Coach silver-fox throw; the mirror is
vintage John Dickinson and the
crackle-lacquer cabinet was designed by Samuel Marx.

ABOVE
Delphine Krakoff designed her daughter's
daybed, and the oak dresser was hand-painted by their friend
the illustrator Pierre Le-Tan.

17

DONATELLA VERSACE

"I'm not a minimalist."

Where does good taste begin and excess leave off? That's one of many questions that come to mind when perusing the Milan apartment of fashion designer Donatella Versace. She has done for interior decoration what Jayne Mansfield did for film: Add equal parts peroxide, hot pink, and leopard print, and then hit the frappé button. "I still remember when I saw the building, it was really powerful," says Versace, who came across the property in the 1980s. "And I love anything powerful. I loved the elevator—it reminds me of the one in *Suddenly, Last Summer.*"

She and her then-husband, Paul Beck, hired the office of tastemaker Renzo Mongiardino to revamp the place (the dining room's Asian-themed mural and exotic tilework still dazzle) and called in the same team as their family grew and they took over the neighboring apartments. The coffered ceilings and geometric floor tiles that are Mongiardino hallmarks unify the spaces, but since then, Versace has gone where no Renzo man has gone before.

"I'm not a minimalist," she says, stating the obvious. Her favorite colors of black and gold are much in evidence, along with leopard spots on blue velvet brocade. And there's a bathroom as big as the Ritz. "Most people would think it was huge, but for me, it can't be big enough," Versace says. Even after the bathroom was finished, she insisted that the workmen make it bigger again and then, on top of that, add a wall of mirror.

The combination of aristocratic elegance in the main rooms and rock-star swagger in the private sanctums might appear at odds, but "I like having both lives," the designer explains. "When I want to have people over and be glamorous, I go downstairs, but now that the children are older, I wanted a place to have some intimacy, where I can entertain a few friends, or be by myself." And a place where she can mix it up to her heart's content. "I don't think many people would do an Oriental bathroom next to a modern bedroom. People think it's not correct. They want one style, so everything matches. But really, that's the most old-fashioned thing you can do, even when it's modern. Behind the modern façades, there are a lot of old-fashioned people."

Does that mean that the history of excess is one of freedom? Probably not many intellectuals would put it that way, but if expressing yourself the way you desire is excessive, then the rule holds. So, Donatella Versace: radical taste activist? Perhaps. As she says when asked what she values most, "Freedom—I love freedom, especially in the mind." ∎

OPPOSITE
A guest room is outfitted
with neoclassical furniture and a lacquered folding
screen from the Art Deco
period. The bedding, curtains, bench,
and rug are by
Versace Home Collection.

ABOVE
A mirror-lined, neoclassical-style
display cabinet in Versace's
bath contains her collection of perfumes. The
painted and gilded
pedestal table is French Empire.

LEFT
A Vanitas chair by Versace Home
Collection, and Versace's
collection of Buddhas, executed in bronze, jade,
and crystal. A mirrored
wall reflects the vaulted ceiling.

RALPH RUCCI

*"There is a conception about luxurious things, that
we have to save them for a time that's right. But an object is only luxurious
if you allow it to be, if you use it."*

At fashion designer Ralph Rucci's jewel box of a penthouse, the fastidious attention to luxury, detail, and exquisite objets d'art is so pronounced that at first glance the effect might seem precious, calculated, even contrived. But when you experience the peace and thoughtfulness of his space, it's clear that those words, though vaguely pejorative, are truly ideals to aim for.

The Manhattan resident is not down-to-earth, nor does he aspire to be. This is a man who named his company, Chadō Ralph Rucci, after the Japanese tea ceremony. Known for his unrepentantly beautiful dresses and suits, he was the first American since Mainbocher invited to present couture under his own name in Paris. He believes that beautiful things—silver Buccellati objects, settees upholstered in ostrich, an Egyptian sculpture fragment—have a meditative quality. It's a concept Rucci has embraced more fully in the years since he found the penthouse and began enriching its rooms. "I am getting more cozy," the onetime minimalist reveals. Nonetheless, remnants of his old restraint are here. "I don't like the idea of clutter," says the designer. "Minimalism has to provide the perfect stage so you can set the furniture and things in a manner that allows you to think, to meditate, to be inspired."

A celebratory take on daily living suffuses Rucci's world. "I love ceremony," he says. "It helps me to get going in the morning. It's in how I set a tray for myself for breakfast, how I read the paper, do yoga, how I dress, how I work." The old-fashioned ethic he calls gentlemanly behavior lends his life a Zenlike peace. "I like cuff links," he says with a laugh. "I like dating. Even my shoe trees are ceremonial. I have a housekeeper more insane than I am: She keeps the sterling flatware beyond polished, and my sheets are always pressed."

Many people who love aesthetics today often apologize for it, as if it's some kind of frivolous weakness. As with the clothes he designs, which, though simple and elegant, make no bones about being refined and flawlessly crafted, Rucci has no qualms about choreographing his life and apartment as if it were a ballet. "I don't think it's pretentious," he says. "There is a conception in this country about luxurious things, that we have to save them for a time that's right. But an object is only luxurious if you allow it to be, if you use it. When you live with beautiful things, you stimulate your mind, you enjoy life a little bit more." Instead of focusing on what he doesn't have—as so many of us do—Rucci concentrates, much more happily, on what he's got. We should all be so shallow. ■

MARY McFADDEN

"My last apartment was Moghul;
this time around I decided on Byzantium."

Given her penchant for melding ancient civilizations into modern wardrobes, it seems fitting that Mary McFadden spent her early childhood in Memphis, Tennessee, a city named for one of the capitals of Pharaonic Egypt. "There may be something in that," says the fashion designer, whose 1973 debut collection—launched after the renegade society deb spent the late 1960s in the former Rhodesia as a *Vogue* editor, a reporter for a left-wing newspaper, and an arts promoter—contained allusions to China, ancient Greece, and tribal Africa.

That cultural wanderlust is reflected in her living spaces. "My last apartment was Moghul," says McFadden, perched on an Egyptian wood stool. "This time around I decided on Byzantium." Theme firmly in mind, she called on artist Joseph Stashkevetch to bedazzle her latest pad, a low-ceilinged, one-bedroom in a nondescript modern building on Manhattan's Upper East Side. She and the artist created extravagant wall stencils that they copied from motifs in four Byzantine churches, including a fourth-century chapel built by Emperor Constantine and the Church of the Savior of the Spilled Blood in St. Petersburg. The work method, however, was unstructured.

As McFadden explains, "We never knew which stencils we would use or in what combination" nor which elements of the previous day's work they would erase. Under a mottled coat of verdigris-color paint, for instance, the faint outlines of a rejected Stashkevetch trompe l'oeil urn can still be seen. "We were two different personae with two different visions," McFadden says, "but each of us wanted to achieve a Byzantine aura."

Golden arabesques dance across the walls. Gilded frames border Tibetan mandalas, portraits of ancient Southeast Asian royalty, and Choson-period gouaches. Overhead, the ceilings are paved with thousands of squares of gossamer gold leaf, some more smoothly applied than others. "We weren't terribly expert," McFadden admits, pointing out the unevenness. "Remember, we did all this in just six months." Their solution to the problem? Silk-screened motifs that tone down the metallic brashness and divert the eyes of visiting perfectionists.

What cultural expedition is next in McFadden's home-decorating future? "Japan is definitely on my shortlist," the designer says. "I saw a Japanese restaurant recently on East 76th Street, and it was so inspiring to me, just the way the façade was painted and the flags were hung." Mr. Stashkevetch, get those stencils ready. ∎

CARLOS SOUZA

"I wanted to start over.
But you can't avoid your past entirely; there were
things I just couldn't part with."

Since his modeling days back in the 1980s, Carlos Souza, the dashing international public-relations director of the House of Valentino, has been part of fashion designer Valentino Garavani's haute-couture kingdom. With his princely manners, affectionate good humor, and effortless joie de vivre, the suave Brazilian has refined the role of PR front man into the art of international social diplomacy while juggling a global itinerary for Valentino at press events and galas. On top of that, Souza has created a line of jewelry, Most Wanted Design, which is sold at chic stores, including Maxfield in L.A., Barneys New York, Browns in London, and Colette in Paris. Its launch coincided with his move to the Piazza Vittorio section of Rome, where artists and gallery owners have revitalized a once-slummy area into what he calls "a cauldron of cultures in a young and ebullient area."

After buying a three-bedroom apartment in an 1860s building, "I threw a bomb," Souza says, an appropriately explosive way to describe the top-to-bottom renovation that was followed by a full-blown edit of everything he owned, an enviable trove of objects, furniture, and art from the States, France, China, Indonesia, and points beyond. "I wanted to start over," says Souza, who did just that by shipping loads of belongings to his house in Rio de Janeiro, where he spends holidays with his sons, Sean and Anthony (he also has a getaway in Nova Friburgo, a mountain town a couple of hours outside of Rio). "But you can't avoid your past entirely," he notes. "There were things I just couldn't part with." A Chinese bed and chair in the sitting room survived the move across the city, taking their place in the sparsely decorated apartment alongside Mies van der Rohe furniture, iron vases from the flea markets in Paris, an Isamu Noguchi paper lamp, and a Javanese bamboo bench. Soon these were joined by new acquisitions: pashmina scarves from Jaipur, Mao Zedong pillows from London, and a medley of blue-and-white Chinese porcelain that greets visitors in the entrance hall.

In the whitewashed dining room is a spare modern table laden with lacquered trays from Hong Kong, jade figurines, and a white-bronze sculpture. The master bedroom holds treasures new and old too: A platform bed by the art director/product designer Fabien Baron holds its own against a Chinese cabinet adorned with Brazilian Madonnas and a baby Jesus from Prague, ethnic necklaces, and vintage cameras. Souza's greatest luxury, however, is the respite his new home offers in a whirlwind world. "Every morning I open all the windows and prepare a cup of green tea as life on the piazza is starting up," he says, "and I feel perfect peace and calm." ∎

INSIDE INFORMATION

■ I travel constantly and am able to shop all over the world for furniture and accessories, fashion and food.

■ My favorite sources include the Old Bazaar in Istanbul for jewelry and antiques; the central market in Denpasar, Bali, for textiles—especially batiks, I love blue-and-white batiks; Stubbs & Wootton in New York, Palm Beach, and Southampton for shoes; Blue Man in Rio for men's swimsuits; incense from Esteban in Paris; and Ito En on Madison Avenue or Mariage Frères in Paris for green tea.

PRECEDING PAGES
Jewelry designer and Valentino PR director
Carlos Souza at his
apartment in Rome's Piazza Vittorio.

Souza pairs a sculptural
Noguchi floor lamp with a Barcelona daybed in the
sitting room; artworks by
Gary Hume and James Brown are displayed
on the mantel.

OPPOSITE
Sleek wood cabinetry contrasts with a
marble-sheathed backsplash
and counters in the dramatic double-height kitchen;
the pendant light fixtures
are a Philippe Starck design for Flos.

ABOVE
The dining room features a table and
chairs by Cappellini,
and photography by Sam Taylor-Wood and
Perry Ogden.

TOP RIGHT
A vintage Le Corbusier chaise
longue is draped with a sari from Jaipur.

BOTTOM RIGHT
A Chinese daybed is the focal point of the
spacious sitting room.

ABOVE
The bathroom is equipped
with a travertine tub and a Bang & Olufsen
stereo system.

RIGHT
Rings, necklaces,
and earrings from Souza's jewelry line,
Most Wanted Design.

OPPOSITE
In the master bedroom, a
platform bed
designed by Fabien Baron for Cappellini is
dressed in Bellora linens;
a 1978 Joe Eula portrait of Souza
hangs on the wall.

RICKY & RALPH LAUREN

"Being on the ocean is important to me, and the house itself just seems to be a part of the dramatic landscape."

Out at the end of Long Island, in a place called Montauk Point, is a house whose cedar-shingle roof is barely visible above a tangle of scrub pines and beach roses. Built in 1940 by Antonin Raymond, who had worked with Frank Lloyd Wright and practiced in Japan, the building has remained virtually unchanged, despite the fact that for decades it has been a home away from home for Ralph Lauren, his wife, Ricky, and their children.

Yes, its interior has been made more sleek with vintage pieces in pale woods and bamboo, rattan and wicker, and lots of crisp linen. The floors and the original golden gum plywood ceilings have been polished, and the walls painted pristine white. But otherwise the house feels like a relic of an earlier era, when summers were about relaxation and the only contact desired was with nature, not via BlackBerry. There also are three small outbuildings: a guesthouse, essentially one skylit room with an adjacent kitchenette; a cottage that contains a great room with an open kitchen flanked by bedrooms for the Laurens' grown children, Andrew, David, and Dylan; and a screening room with a tiny kitchen for whipping up popcorn. "We do watch a lot of movies in the screening room," says the fashion designer, adding, "Film has always been such an important part of my life and a major inspiration."

All the buildings on the family's compound are within a few hundred feet of each other. Even when you throw in the secluded pool, down a gentle slope and sheltered by pines and rhododendrons, the property can hardly be considered ostentatious. The low ceilings, warm woods, rugged dunes, and twisted pines bring to mind the photographs of Edward Weston and Ansel Adams (a connection reiterated by Ricky Lauren's own moody images). The family primarily uses the place during the summer, says the designer, "but I stay there, on occasion, year-round. There is something serene and rejuvenating about being there during the winter, when the air is so crisp."

Ralph Lauren is the quintessential American tastemaker, and he understands that there is a strain of modesty in the American character. For him, maxims about leaving well enough alone and if it ain't broke, don't fix it still apply. "Being on the ocean is important to me," he says, "and the house itself just seems to be a part of the dramatic landscape. The scenery from every inch of this property, and from every room, is beautiful. The dunes of Montauk and the vast horizon are breathtaking." And as he's wise enough to know, sometimes that's enough. ∎

PRECEDING PAGES
Teak chaise longues with crisp Ralph Lauren Home
denim–covered cushions offer
a view of the rock-edged swimming pool; the striped
towels are vintage Ralph Lauren.

In the living room of the main
house, cyprus club chairs and a built-in sofa are covered in
Ralph Lauren Home linen; the tray
ceiling is sheathed in polished gum plywood.

OPPOSITE
Identically framed photographs of the Laurens and
their children are casually
arranged on a wall in the den of the main house.
RIGHT
Near the cottage that is
used by the Laurens' children, two teak chaise longues are
positioned to take in the Atlantic seascape.

BELOW
Vintage Bertoia wire chairs
underscore the low-key but stylish air of the stone-walled
kitchen in the guesthouse;
the tableware is by Ralph Lauren Home.

ABOVE
A gnarled black-cherry tree grows near
the swimming pool.

OPPOSITE
The living room of the guesthouse
features rattan armchairs
and a linen-clad sofa. A polished-nickel
mirror hangs above a
driftwood mantel set into a rough-cut
Montauk-stone chimney.

ABOVE
Bluestone and wood
were used to sheathe the bathing alcove
in the guesthouse.

RIGHT
Family photographs
decorate the dressing area adjacent to
the master bedroom.

OPPOSITE
In the master bedroom, a custom-
made teak tester bed
is hung with sheer white cotton by
Ralph Lauren Home.

KENNETH JAY LANE

The evocatively layered, highly Proustian digs where jewelry designer Kenneth Jay Lane has lived for 30-odd years takes up the core of a townhouse on Manhattan's Park Avenue, a creation of turn-of-the-century architect Stanford White. Virtually all its original details remain intact. One enters a complex, beautifully appointed foyer, where the soaring walls are painted in subtly varying shades of red. Circular mirrors reflect light above a pair of faux-painted burled-walnut doors. A slender staircase rises to a balcony and the bedroom, and beneath the balcony, a third door opens to reveal the velvety, robber-baron splendor of Lane's famously sumptuous drawing room.

The duplex apartment, however, is not furnished like a period house, though the eclectic array of art and objects does capture the stylish decadence of the 1890s. The silver-haired designer is a connoisseur of European furniture and objets d'art and an authority on Orientalist paintings. Says Lane, "After I bought two, I was hooked."

The drawing room is not only a reflection of his wide-ranging knowledge, obsessive antiquing, and taste for ethnic curiosities; it has developed, after three decades of honing and refining, into a true reflection of his personality. The contents are constantly being rearranged to make certain each new acquisition finds its perfect place, and this perpetual reevaluation lends the room its cosmopolitan atmosphere and recaptures the elusive spirit of a less vulgar age.

The drawing room is a cozy cocoon in the center of the workaholic capital of the world. Oversize tasseled banquettes are piled with cushions, and here and there are plush ottomans, Persian carpets, leopard patterns, and Kang-Hsi pots overflowing with orchids and palms. The elaborate clutter serves as a theatrical backdrop for entertaining a seemingly endless crowd of friends and acquaintances. The designer's guest lists encompass a fascinating universe of diverse personalities: boldface names from the entertainment world, American tycoons, and café society, as well as soigné representatives of London's smart set. As in so many other things, Lane's taste in friends is catholic.

There are times when this distinguished man-about-town plays at being a snob and a dilettante. Frankly, he is neither. His suave personality, his luxurious surroundings, and his sense of humor lead one to forget that he started life with no advantages. What he has achieved—in business and the arts and in his incomparable *savoir-vivre*—all are great accomplishments. And they are his alone. ■

INSIDE INFORMATION

■ Why do people talk about hanging art? It's hanging pictures. My drawing room is decorated with Orientalist paintings. They are hung salon-style, like in an old-fashioned gallery, so some are displayed quite high. You don't have to have everything right in front of your nose.

■ Picture lights can illuminate an entire room, but only use them for paintings, not drawings under glass, because of the glare. If you don't like to see the cord, just wrap it with tape or ribbon the color of the wall, but I don't bother. If a picture is hung high, the light should be installed at the bottom of the frame, facing up, because it's easier to get at the bulb when it needs changing.

■ I never think about color, but things have to live together in a certain way. I wouldn't put a Cézanne over a Rothko, but maybe a Picasso would work, depending on which period of Picasso. A late Picasso would be better.

PRECEDING PAGES
Jewelry designer Kenneth Jay Lane
strikes a pose amid the
Orientalist paintings of his legendary drawing
room, which is located
in a historic Stanford White–designed
brownstone on Park Avenue.

OPPOSITE
The drawing room is furnished
with a 19th-century
English Regency table, Louis XV needlework-
covered chairs, and
an 18th-century glass-front Boulle
bookcase; the intricate
architectural detail is original
to the building.

TOP RIGHT
A 19th-century light fixture is suspended
above a tapestry-strewn sofa.

CENTER RIGHT
A mezzanine library
overlooks the dining area's George IV table
and Regency side chairs.

BOTTOM RIGHT
The bedroom's woodwork
was inspired by the library of the British
embassy in Paris.

TAMARA MELLON

When word got out that Tamara Mellon, the founder and president of the shoe-and-accessories empire Jimmy Choo, was christening her new London flat with a dinner party, the uninvited started calling in such rapid succession that the guest list jumped from 20 to 50. Among those who made the cut: Sarah, Duchess of York, Claire Danes, Quincy Jones, and Formula One–racing tycoon Flavio Briatore. "It was so much fun, no one wanted to leave," sighs Mellon.

That her buddies—especially her fabulous and famous friends—would be interested in Mellon's latest home should not be surprising. After all, she is known for her trendsetting taste. Another potential source of curiosity could be the unexpected Notting Hill address that Mellon has selected for herself and her young daughter, Araminta. Though long a Chelsea habitué, she was entranced by the Edwardian charm of the sprawling apartment. So was her interior designer, Martyn Lawrence-Bullard, a man renowned for getting a bead on a client's personality.

Nowhere has he done this better than in the enormous living room. Two impossibly chic raspberry velvet sofas, scattered with effervescent lime-green silk pillows, sit on a huge leopard-print rabbit-skin rug. Verner Panton sconces made of Capiz shell, mirrored consoles, and Murano-glass lamps add to the quirky, offbeat atmosphere. "I wanted to reflect Tamara's great sense of style," says Lawrence-Bullard. "She did not care what period each piece was from as long as everything had good, strong lines." Mellon's art collection goes a long way toward defining the apartment's looks, too. The range of works is eye-poppingly diverse: Damien Hirst spin paintings, fashion photography by Bill King and Horst P. Horst, an Andy Warhol print of Grace Kelly, a Jean-Michel Basquiat.

If the living room is the formal party area, ready for an invasion of duchesses and the like, the master bedroom is the flat's sanctuary, furnished with exotica like an 18th-century embroidered tapestry from Istanbul and a mother-of-pearl-inlaid chest from Syria. Some visitors, however, think the real treasure is the shoe room stocked with Jimmy Choos. Mellon has a separate closet just for jeans, and a London firm color-coordinates her clothes seasonally.

It's all pretty luxe here in this part of Notting Hill, but Mellon's favorite spot is the television room she calls her snug. "If I have people over, it's usually a buffet and quite relaxed," says London's undisputed glamour girl. "I love the idea of having a television area with a huge sofa where people can just lounge around. It's great fun." ∎

PRECEDING PAGES
Tamara Mellon in the living
room of her apartment in Notting Hill. A Damien Hirst
painting hangs above the fireplace.

TOP LEFT
Vintage campaign-style chairs by Jacques
Adnet are used in the dining area.
The 1930s mirrored console is by Serge Roche, and the
photo is by Jim Lee.

ABOVE
Mellon's shoe closet holds more than
400 pairs of Jimmy Choos.

LEFT
In the office is a Warhol
print of Grace Kelly. The Louis XVI–style steel desk
is by Jansen, and the 1960s
Eames desk chair is upholstered in a hot-pink
Edelman leather.

OPPOSITE
In the master bedroom, an 18th-
century Ottoman tapestry is displayed behind the
bed; the pillows and bed skirt are made
of custom-embroidered fabric
by the Silk Trading Co., and the lacquered side
cabinets are 1940s French.

PRECEDING PAGES
An 18th-century Persian horse, gilded antiques,
and sofas strewn with silk shawls
nestle under the living room's beamed ceiling.

OPPOSITE
A 1940s daybed cushioned
with red velvet and pony-skin on the
stone-walled veranda.

RIGHT
Fashion designer Roberto Cavalli
and his wife, creative
director and former beauty queen Eva Duringer,
pause on the herringbone-
brick path that leads to their house.

BELOW
A seating area equipped
with zebra hides and zebra-print cushions and
towels occupies one end
of the indoor swimming pool.

ABOVE
One of Duringer's signature eclectic
table settings, replete
with specimen orchids, a branch of red coral,
and rose-pattern plates and
leopard-print napkins from the Roberto
Cavalli Home Collection.

RIGHT
A Florentine marble table
in the crimson sitting room displays Duringer's
collection of spheres, marble eggs,
and mirrored-glass globes. The cushions
are made of dyed fur.

OPPOSITE
A 19th-century gilt-wood
mirror serves as a headboard in the villa's
master bedroom.

TEMPLE ST. CLAIR CARR

"I have to go to Marrakech!
I can't just buy a rug without an adventure attached."

With her proper Southern upbringing, penchant for escape, and novel-perfect name, Temple St. Clair Carr is the kind of woman Henry James might have immortalized as a heroine. She certainly has the cheekbones. If only she had a tragic flaw and fragile sensibility to match. But as fate would have it, Carr has sidestepped Jamesian pitfalls such as consumption and arranged marriages to run the 21-year-old jewelry firm Temple St. Clair. While living in Florence after college, she asked a local artisan to fabricate a few Renaissance-inspired jewels. Then the young entrepreneur began incorporating ancient coins into her creations, and a business—and lifestyle—was born.

Carr uses the word *classic* to describe her work, but there's whimsy, too. The same contrast is on view in the townhouse on Manhattan's Lower East Side that she shares with her husband and business partner, Paul Engler, and their young sons, Alexander and Archer. The 19th-century building looks simple and romantic from the outside. Inside, however, is a bit of a surprise, a deft, evocative edit of modern, antique, Occidental, and Oriental. The modern backgrounds resulted from necessity: The couple discovered that the aged building had to be gutted because of major structural problems, so they decided to rebuild in a clean, spare style. "We didn't want anything too precious," says Carr, who turned for help to architect Steven Harris. "We wanted it to be livable, not ostentatious."

The challenge for Harris lay in some of the building's defects. "The floors pitched downward almost a foot," says the architect, his alarm still registering years later. "It was completely unsound." One of his solutions was to install a freestanding, boxed spiral stairway that didn't require the support of the uneven brick walls. Another (literally) bright idea was the bank of industrial-steel windows at the rear of the house that keeps the rooms full of light.

Modern interventions aside, the interiors seem to take their cues from a worn Baedeker, being all fragments and memories. There are family photographs of one of Carr's grandmothers in front of the Pyramids, a few chairs from her childhood home in Virginia, a bone from the skeleton of a sea turtle that she found in Bali, a painted dresser from the designer's postgraduate sojourn amid the romantic domes and stucco of Florence. The rooms are about experience rather than decorating, says Carr. "My mother keeps telling me I need a carpet for one room. But I reply, 'I have to go to Marrakech! I can't just buy a rug without an adventure attached.' " ■

PRECEDING PAGES
*Jewelry designer Temple St. Clair Carr
with her German shepherd,
Daisy, at the Manhattan townhouse she shares
with her husband and two sons.*

ABOVE
*The dining room is furnished with
a marble-top Saarinen Tulip table, vintage
French lamps, and a chandelier
and antique chairs from Carr's childhood
home in Virginia.*

RIGHT
*Heirloom china and
tableware from Europe are stowed in an
antique French cupboard.*

OPPOSITE
*The living room's 19th-century
sofa is upholstered with fabric brought back
from Florence; the
paintings are by Caio Fonseca.*

OPPOSITE
The kitchen features Carrara-marble
counters and a custom-made
stainless-steel hood and storage unit; the
range is by Wolf.

ABOVE
The antique French
desk in the study belonged to Carr's
grandmother.

LEFT
Temple St. Clair jewelry is displayed on an
antique Florentine chest.

OPPOSITE
Carr had the Shaker-style bed custom
made, and uses an antique suzani as a bedcover; the 19th-century tea
table belonged to her great-grandmother.

ABOVE
In Alexander and Archer's
room, the children's beds are dressed in Indian quilts, and the
carpets are Pakistani.

GIAMBATTISTA VALLI

"I don't shop. I buy things that inspire me,
that give me emotion."

For more than three centuries the best and brightest of England and the Continent have headed to Rome. The artists who won the prestigious Prix de Rome and the young aristocratic dandies who hired them to do their portraits in the 1870s, jet-setters in search of a bit of la dolce vita in the 1960s, and the hordes of cell-phone-wielding exchange students landing at Fiumicino today have all looked to the ancient city as a source of artistic inspiration. But what of the young and talented who actually grow up in Rome? Where does their Grand Tour take them? For Giambattista Valli, the answer was obvious. Go East, young Roman.

The designer—a former creative director of Emanuel Ungaro's prêt-à-porter collection, he struck out on his own in 2004—has traveled in that direction frequently, carrying on a long-term love affair with India, Turkey, Japan, and Indonesia. And he's brought back some amazing finds. "I don't shop," Valli announces. "I buy things that inspire me, that give me emotion." Many of these items are on display in his pied-à-terre, which isn't far from the house in which he was raised. An antique Chinese wood bowl sits beside a 1970s steel-and-leather table in the entrance hall. In the living room, a bulbous Noguchi light sculpture perches next to a 1950s horn chair from Texas, and hanging above an 18th-century Rajasthani settee is a Francis Bacon rendering of a tortured soul. A half-dozen Marilyn Monroes by Andy Warhol smile down from an adjacent wall. In Valli's bedroom, where a colorful antique suzani from Turkey covers the bed, worn 19th-century Indonesian carved-wood doors are fashioned into an ad hoc headboard.

The whole amalgam—a little bit hip, a little bit hippie, a smidgen of Zen, and a dollop of rock and roll—is a perfect metaphor for both Valli's life and his designs. "I like things that are kind of eclectic, when one thing doesn't go with another," he says. When he found the 1,500-square-foot apartment, "there were rooms and rooms, and walls all over." To help Valli clarify that off-putting warren, he turned to a friend, architect Luigi Scialanga. "I wanted a beautiful white box that I could put things in," the designer recalls. Scialanga delivered—tearing down some walls, opening others, and painting the rooms white for a loftlike effect that's given just enough patina by the original wood beams. "The apartment was nice before, but Luigi transformed it into an amazing place," Valli adds. "And I like that it doesn't look too Roman. It really feels international." ■

PRECEDING PAGES
Artworks by Francis Bacon and Andy Warhol
are displayed in the living room.

LEFT
Giambattista Valli sits below a bust of Constantine
the Great in the courtyard
of the Palazzo dei Conservatori in Rome.

ABOVE
An Isamu Noguchi light sculpture and a 1950s
horn chair in the living room.

OPPOSITE
The steel-and-wood staircase
was designed by Francesco Antilici. Arne Jacobsen
chairs flank a leather-and-
chrome table by Willy Rizzo; the paper lamp
is a first-edition Noguchi.

OPPOSITE
An antique Turkish suzani is spread
across the bed in Valli's
wood-ceilinged guest room; Spider, a 1996
drawing by Antonio
Pierri, leans against the wall.

ABOVE
In Valli's bedroom, 19th-
century Indonesian carved-wood doors
serve as an atmospheric
headboard. The watercolor is by
Alberto Pasini.

LEFT
The bath, which is sheathed
in Carrara marble, has a templelike air,
reinforced by accessories
such as sake cups, an elephant sculpture from
Jaipur, and a Japanese bonsai-
tree sculpture.

ANGEL SANCHEZ

*"When friends arrive, I don't know
what happens. Suddenly everyone feels very sexy, and
an hour later it's a party."*

La vida Caracas follows certain patterns. So does much of the city's decor. Grown-ups, young and old, favor solidity over swank, like Oriental rugs and 18th-century antiques or reasonable facsimiles. So when Angel Sanchez opened the front door of his mountainside duplex, eyebrows were raised at its 007 sizzle: scarlet walls, fur carpets, mod American furniture. Corporate Caracas types think it's all a bit much, but even they are willing to make allowances. After all, Sanchez says with a laugh, "I'm a fashion designer."

His head shaved aerodynamically smooth, his rock-solid chin graced with a goatee, Sanchez is the hottest Venezuelan export since Carolina Herrera. He and a posse of friends bought property in Altamira, a low-rise neighborhood that is perched on one of the tree-covered hills that ring the capital city's skyscrapered downtown. There they constructed a Richard Meier–esque building containing six spacious apartments. Sanchez took half of the two top floors and promptly called New York designer Christopher Coleman, a longtime friend, to choreograph his glass-walled aerie, which is the work of Caracas architect Totón Sánchez, another of the fashion designer's pals.

Coleman persuaded Sanchez to ditch his aesthetic daydream of beige, white, and brown and embrace the good vibrations of deep red. And how about 1950s and '60s pieces instead of contemporary furniture? Before Sanchez really had much of a chance to object, in came a low-slung sofa wrapped in Hermès-orange vinyl, with velvet cushions to match. A pair of T. H. Robsjohn-Gibbings wood armchairs and a womblike desk chair completed the seating in the living area. Coleman pointed out that a white flokati would make an ideal visual transition from the apartment's snowy marble floor to the warmer tones of the living area's furnishings. Sanchez was not convinced, but, the ebullient Venezuelan recalls, "When we laid it out, I said, 'Wow. You're right.' "

Emboldened, Sanchez commissioned red accent walls downstairs and yellow for the hall leading to the roof terrace. The bedroom, however, conforms more closely to his original preferences. The headboard is made of gleaming dark wenge, and the formfitting cushions of an iron chair are covered in cowhide that he used for handbags. Underneath it all is a rug of fox pelts. "When I'm by myself, it's a very contemplative space," the designer says. "But when friends arrive, I don't know what happens. Suddenly everyone feels very sexy, and an hour later it's a party." ■

PRECEDING PAGES
Angel Sanchez created the Lucite
desk in a corner of his
Caracas bedroom for a local AIDS benefit; the
patchwork leather
ottoman is by De Sede.

LEFT
Interior decorator Christopher
Coleman designed the
living room banquette in Hermès-orange vinyl and
found the vintage
Robsjohn-Gibbings armchairs;
the flokati rug adds softness to the snowy
marble flooring.

ABOVE
Fashion designer Angel Sanchez.

OPPOSITE
Coleman designed a
colorful runner to echo the bathroom's
inset-glass ceiling.

ABOVE
The terrace offers a dramatic
view of downtown Caracas; the Sunbrella-
fabric privacy screen was
designed by architect Totón Sánchez.

TOP RIGHT
Sanchez commissioned
a wenge bench to match the Parsons-style
dining table; the
artwork is by Juan García de Cubas.

RIGHT
Sanchez's bed features a wenge
headboard with a pivoting
side panel and linens by Calvin Klein Home;
the chair is upholstered in
a cowhide used for handbags, and the
rug is made of fox pelts
from a supplier to the designer's
fur collection.

MARIA BEATRICE & LEONARDO FERRAGAMO

When Maria Beatrice Garagnani agreed to marry fashion-house scion Leonardo Ferragamo nearly 20 years ago, she knew she would be making some lifestyle adjustments. What she didn't expect was the fact that she wouldn't be choosing her own home. Instead, her fiancé presented her with a house as a marital fait accompli: Villa Le Rose, a 15th-century mansion near Florence whose enormity was hardly the blushing bride's style.

Though she had some serious reservations, "It's a treat to live in a house with such great architectural and historical qualities," says Villa Le Rose's present chatelaine, whose tumbling curls give her a cinquecento air. Still, it hasn't been all mink. "Leonardo handed it over to me quite empty. It was my duty to put in all the furniture and stuff."

In 2004, after more than a decade of loving wear and tear had become obvious—the Ferragamos now have four children and maintain a working farm of chickens, turkeys, and other livestock—the house underwent a major renovation at the hands of Maria Beatrice's sisters Elena Garagnani, an artist, and Francesca Garagnani Poccianti, a designer, and Francesca's architect husband, Carlo Ludovico Poccianti. Elena and her craftsmen restored the extraordinary collection of murals, ranging from frolicsome Fragonard-style landscapes in the dining room to neo-Pompeian arabesques in an upstairs bath. As for a fantastic double-height chamber that is used as the family's main living room, Francesca smartly outfitted it with tailored sofas and button-tufted ottomans of sapphire silk velvet and polished tables laden with masses of blue-and-white porcelain. At the center of this rapturous space, its walls given over to Piranesian scenes depicting classical ruins, is a king-size cocktail table of smoky travertine.

"It's a big aristocratic house, but we didn't want the rooms to feel old," says Francesca of the modern intrusions. "We wanted a certain amount of freshness." Whimsy was welcome too. The fanciful chinoiserie murals in one of the guest rooms, for example, sparked the creation of a pagoda-peak silk canopy to crown the bed.

Lyrical hand-painting and heirloom glamour aside, bedazzled visitors are quickly brought back to reality by the daily nine-to-five. Maria Beatrice gets down and dirty in the kitchen garden, and she also keeps a watchful eye on all those chickens. "Picking the wrong hen for lunch would be a tragedy," she says, laughing. "We have to be very careful that we don't accidentally cook one that the children are raising." ■

PRECEDING PAGES
The main living room of Villa Le Rose
is furnished with blue silk
velvet sofas, a 1970s travertine cocktail table,
and a floor lamp made
from an 18th-century candleholder.

OPPOSITE
The Pompeian-style frescoes that
animate the walls of
one of the salons were added in the 18th century.
The painted Italian
sofa and gilt-wood armchairs also
date from the 1700s.

ABOVE
The approach to the Ferragamos'
house, which was built
in the 15th century for a member of the Antinori
wine family, is a drive
shaded by an allée of cypress trees.

OPPOSITE
*In the dining room, murals depict
a pastoral scene; the
mahogany-and-walnut table, upholstered
chairs, gilt-wood console,
and Murano-glass chandelier are all
18th century.*

RIGHT
*The kitchen's Tuscan-style
fireplace is original to the house. The chairs
are Spanish, and the
overscale light fixture was made
by local craftsmen.*

BELOW
*The 1950s pool is ringed by a hedge
of scalloped boxwoods that
have been clipped to echo the silhouette of
a stucco-covered wall.*

ABOVE
High-relief plaster figures
encircle the Ferragamos' library. The
burl-wood desk
is a 19th-century antique.

RIGHT
A painted sink vanity
echoes the wall decorations in one of
the villa's bathrooms.

OPPOSITE
An elaborately draped gilt-wood
baldachin dating
from the 17th century surmounts
a guest room bed.

INSIDE INFORMATION

■ To us, lofts should be clutter-free, open spaces. We can't imagine dividing a loft into small rooms or dropping the ceilings; and we prefer a neutral palette as a backdrop, accented by punches of color.

■ We entertain frequently, and like to create a sense of intimacy—even in this big space—where guests can flirt, joke, and recline languorously.

■ Flowers, candles, and music are carefully selected for each occasion. We always ensure that there are enough waiters for the crowd; guests should never have to wait for a drink. And we love serving Champagne, or a signature cocktail like an Earl Grey martini.

PRECEDING PAGES
Ranjana and Naeem Khan in the living room
of their SoHo loft.

OPPOSITE
A low-slung velvet sofa by
Minotti and an overscale tufted-leather ottoman
by De Padova give
the living area a loungelike feel.

ABOVE
A mahoni table and rustic teak
bench by Andrianna Shamaris in the dining
area; the photograph is by Peter Beard.

TOP RIGHT
A mirrored wall sculpture acts as
a headboard in the master
bedroom; the bedcover and pillows were
custom made by Naeem Khan
Home, and the Lightolier chandelier is
from the 1960s.

BOTTOM RIGHT
Colorful "Diamond Dust Shoe"
prints by Andy Warhol
and Vernon Panton Globe ceiling lights
grace the living room.

ZANG TOI

*"I didn't want to just tear a page out of history; I wanted it to
be French but done in a modern way."*

Paris in New York. Such a simple, seductive phrase, especially for a Francophile who daydreams of the Right Bank while traipsing through midtown Manhattan. Those four tempting little words, appearing in a real-estate advertisement, were all it took to get the Malaysia-born fashion designer Zang Toi into the first available taxi. "I fell in love with it immediately," Toi says of his new place, a gracious apartment with airy rooms and elaborate moldings that had been carved out of an old mansion on a quiet Upper East Side block. "It has good bones."

The designer briefly considered dressing his 1,300-square-foot digs in a similar color scheme as his previous home, which was a red-and-gold ode to haute chinoiserie. This time around, however, he wanted to create a reverie that would be worthy of Marie Antoinette. "But I didn't want to just tear a page out of history," he says. "I wanted it to be French but done in a modern way." So out went the timeworn gilding and in came a minimalist palette of black, white, and silver. It took an army of painters three full weeks to finish the walls with half a dozen layers of high-gloss white. The parquet floors got three coats of glossy black enamel. Then Toi set about filling the apartment with some handsome antiques, including a glittering circa-1890 Baccarat chandelier in the living room and Louis XVI Revival furniture upholstered in sultry mink-trimmed charcoal cashmere. And he flanked the main fireplace with life-size contemporary portraits of the doomed French queen, which he commissioned from Natasha Zupan.

When Toi fell for a museum-quality bed that had been designed by François Linke, an eminent Belle Epoque cabinetmaker, he wanted it to toe the chromatic line as well. So he did something inspired. Or outrageous, depending on how you feel about the treatment of top-notch antiques. He found a (very reluctant) furniture restorer to refinish the enormous mahogany frame in layers of shining black paint and to silver-plate its golden ormolu.

Though Toi once was comfortable among plentiful objects and elaborate decoration, he is now on a strict diet of minimalism. He lives without a dining table or a guest room. He keeps most of his clothes at his studio, and there isn't an item of clutter on view. Small wonder his sister once asked, "Is this a museum?" In fact, when friends or family do drop by with luggage in hand, Toi has been known to flee to the Carlyle hotel for the duration. "Nothing bothers me more than disorder," he says. "When I come home after a long day, this place puts me in a good mood." ∎

PRECEDING PAGES
Zang Toi's living room is
furnished with a
Louis XVI Revival salon suite upholstered
in Loro Piana cashmere,
and a late-19th-century Baccarat chandelier;
the Marie Antoinette
portraits flanking the fireplace are
by Natasha Zupan.

TOP LEFT
The cabinet in the living room
holds silver-framed
family portraits; the marble-top table was
refinished with white paint,
and the parquet floor was painted
high-gloss black.

ABOVE
Fashion designer Zang Toi.

LEFT
The marble-sheathed bathroom features
a pedestal sink and a
late-19th-century bronze mirror.

OPPOSITE
Léron linens dress Toi's antique
mahogany bed, which
he transformed with shining black paint; the
19th-century chandelier
is ornamented with silver-plate
instruments.

LIZA BRUCE

"Many people think of India as a spiritual place, but I haven't found anything particularly spiritual. I just love the madness."

Liza Bruce and Nicholas Alvis Vega's apartment in Jaipur is so exuberant that it seems as if children had been put in charge of the decoration. Each room is painted a different bold color: hot pink, bright orange, lime-green. Shimmering sequined pillows and patterned rugs are scattered across the stone floors, an invitation to sit and behold interiors that Bruce describes as "raw energy hitting you like helium." And flowers are everywhere: yards and yards of made-to-measure garlands of roses, marigolds, and jasmine. "We sleep and eat near them, even wear them," she says. "Flowers are usually such a luxury, but in India they are very inexpensive, so you feel like you can be extravagant."

India is not exactly a hotbed for second-home real estate among Westerners, unless perhaps you're an eclectic, creative type with a nomadic mentality—a description that fits the London-based fashion designer and her husband, a painter and jewelry designer, to a tee. They discovered the apartment—once the men's quarters of an 1880 mansion by architect Sir Samuel Swinton Jacob, the chief engineer for Jaipur—at a time when old buildings were under assault by modernizing homeowners. "We got here just in time," says Bruce.

Outdoor living is fundamental to their subcontinental reverie. Rooftops, for example, are often the domain of Indian women—a private place to relax without being seen. To create a shelter on their own roof, Bruce and Alvis Vega erected a large red tent. "Tents are a big part of Indian lifestyle," explains Bruce. "It's where hunting parties gather and weddings are held." The red tent also is where the couple sleeps. "Bedrooms are our least favorite place," she says. "We always have futons that can be pushed to the side rather than having a bed control the room." Meals, too, are often alfresco, usually consumed in the cactus-filled roof garden or on the veranda. They also are frequently shared with unexpected guests: wild monkeys. "Monkeys are all over India," says Bruce. "If we leave the table just for a few moments, they will come down and help themselves to pineapple. They are very shrewd."

Living in Jaipur, even part-time, has had a profound effect. "India lifted us to another level," Bruce says, "where we could still function as designers but do it in a way where there's no office, no employees, only other artists we collaborate with." It's an unconventional live-work approach, but it works. As she adds, "Many people think of India as a spiritual place, but I haven't found anything particularly spiritual. I just love the madness." ■

PRECEDING PAGES
Fashion designer Liza Bruce
in the living room of her
apartment in Jaipur. It is housed within
an 1880 mansion by
Sir Samuel Swinton Jacob.

OPPOSITE
Glossy white chairs designed by
Bruce and her husband,
Nicholas Alvis Vega, stand in the study/
library. Blown-glass spheres
are tucked into the over-door niches; the
lime-green wall
treatment is based on traditional
Indian pigments.

TOP RIGHT
White-painted polyhedrons,
mercury-glass spheres,
and a mirror-top table decorate the lavender
veranda; the ceiling's
design is original to the building.

CENTER RIGHT
Golden hand-painted vines frame the doors
and niches of the entrance hall.

BOTTOM RIGHT
Bruce's husband created the
floral motifs in the
meditation room; an Anglo-Indian marble
mantelpiece serves as a
headboard, and the cushion covers
are made of saris.

ARC

DESIGN &
HITECTURE

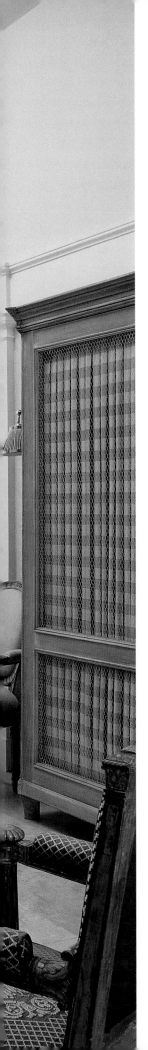

INSIDE INFORMATION

■ Beds should be luxurious, which to me means a complex mix of textures and patterns that are interesting. I always start with top-quality cotton sheets—usually by Porthault or Nancy Koltes—and a down duvet and pillows, and then layer an antique textile or an exotic bedcover hand-embroidered in India or Morocco. A bed should be pristine, but also inviting; dressed but not precious. I don't understand people who have to remove stacks of decorative pillows each night just to go to sleep.

■ I designed this house for easy entertaining, and what I've enjoyed most is planning small dinners in nearly every main room, or in the garden, depending on the season and the number of people invited. We do use the dining room regularly, but I also have casual suppers on the low table in the library or set up brunch in the sunroom. We dine under the pergola all the time. It's more intimate for guests to have a special table set for them, and it makes me appreciate my place even more.

■ Luxury at home involves other senses beyond the visual. For example, my entire house is wired for music, including underwater speakers in the pool. And indoor-outdoor living is one of the best things about L.A. Most of our rooms have doors that lead to a terrace or the garden, which we often leave open so the fresh scent of the lawn can waft in; the fragrance from simply arranged garden roses is subtle but pervasive. Even the smell of Murphy oil soap and good English furniture wax seems luxurious to me. The sense of real life in a house; that's luxury.

LEFT
The marble-floored sunroom
opens onto a terrace;
the mother-of-pearl–encrusted Japanese table
was found in Brussels,
and the ceiling lantern is by Jamb.

TOP RIGHT
Meals are often taken outdoors
at a Baroque-style
stone table; the terrace is paved in Turkish
travertine.

CENTER RIGHT
Smith outfitted the library
with an antique Dutch screen depicting
chinoiserie scenes.

BOTTOM RIGHT
A Beatrice Caracciolo painting
is propped on the
entrance-hall mantel; the fireplace tools are
early-19th-century English.

OPPOSITE
The hemlock-paneled master bedroom
is anchored by a custom-made
canopy bed; the bed curtains are made of a floral
hemp from the Jasper
collection by Michael S. Smith, and the
linens are by D. Porthault.

ABOVE
The master bathroom's bathtub and
fittings are from Smith's
Town collection for Kallista; towels are stowed
on an antique ebonized trolley.

LEFT
In a guest bedroom, a painting by
Peter Paul Rubens
fills one linen-clad wall; the chandelier is
a Smith design.

MURIEL
BRANDOLINI

*"I like to set people free. I give them a hint and encourage them
to let go with their imaginations;
it is the only way that new things can come true."*

On a street of clipped hedges and gleaming brass knockers, interior decorator Muriel Brandolini's townhouse on the Upper East Side of Manhattan offers an unexpected riot of wisteria vines and glass-paneled doors lined with lushly embroidered but tattered silk. Inside, the departure from staid tradition is even more striking. The home she shares with her husband, Nuno, a private investor whose great-grandfather cofounded Fiat, and their children, Brando and Filippa, is in a state of constant upheaval. Brandolini often changes the decor even as the atmosphere of embellished comfort remains constant. The influence of a childhood spent in Indochina is subtle but pervasive—in the budding greens of the parlor floor, the wilderness of ferns at a window, the hand-embroidered silk lanterns. "For me, decorating is very much connected to my memories of Vietnam," says the designer, who lived in Saigon until 1972. "Even during the war, people were always positive. They take life lightheartedly. There's a kind of kitsch, too, in the extreme ornament of its 19th-century temples. And I even put a little bit of that in my work."

This latest incarnation of her home was a true rethinking. "You grow up. Your state of mind requires something else: more warmth, more sophistication," she says. "Before was right for before." Consider the dining room, its once-purple walls now covered in a luminous pewter-green silk that was hand-stitched with fanciful flowers and Asian motifs in pink, dark red, and glints of silver. In contrast, the dining table is composed of industrial steel; it was made by Martin Szekely, an artisan with whom she frequently collaborates. Louis XV dining chairs and a hugely inviting 19th-century daybed offset the contemporary cool of the table.

Throughout the house, unconventional wall treatments establish the mood. Fabrics cover most, along with hand-mixed paint, or even mirrors. The media/guest room is a patchwork of colored straw, and Brandolini's study is lined with a deep-blue fine-wale corduroy. "It's so very dark and rich, but at the same time sporty," says the designer, who also upholstered banquettes in a signature patchwork of vintage Japanese, French, and Indian silks. Often it is not her own work but a piece by another admired talent that she credits for a room's updated look—a rotund cocktail table created by Mattia Bonetti, a fanciful chinoiserie armoire designed for her by Louis Bofferding. Collaboration is vital to Brandolini's work. "I like to set people free. I give them a hint and encourage them to let go with their imaginations," she says, adding with a laugh, "It is the only way that new things can come true." ∎

INSIDE INFORMATION

▪ My style is very impulsive; I don't analyze it. My first instinct is always the right one, and everything has to be fresh in my mind. Why waste time?

▪ I mix all my own paint colors. I don't believe in using paint straight from a can; I can get the results I want directly on the wall.

▪ Wall treatments establish a mood for a house. I use paint, fabrics, and mirrors, but I hate wallpaper; I find it cold.

▪ When a room is small, trying to gain height by leaving a white ceiling is a mistake. I often apply grass cloth on the ceilings as well as the walls, or use a patchwork of patterned fabrics. If the ends don't meet cleanly, border the panels with ribbon. It creates a framework that both defines and unifies the space. Just make a small room a box; it's cozier.

PRECEDING PAGES
Muriel Brandolini in the entrance hall of her Manhattan townhouse. The cast-bronze table is by Michele Oka Doner, the inlaid side chair is Victorian, and the hand-embroidered silk lantern was made in Vietnam.

OPPOSITE
A chandelier made of glass, rock crystal, jade, and pearls illuminates the living room. The podlike cocktail table is a Mattia Bonetti design, and the large painting is a work by Ross Bleckner.

ABOVE
Vintage fabrics cover the settees in Brandolini's ink-blue study; the table is by Ronan & Erwan Bouroullec.

OPPOSITE
In the kitchen, an Ingo Maurer
light fixture
contrasts with a 1940s marble table by
Jean Dunand. The
cabinets are faced with zinc.

RIGHT
The media/guest room features
turn-of-the-century
painted armchairs and a Pop Art–style
rug by Fedora Design. The
ceiling is covered
with vintage silk sari fabric.

BELOW
A 1780s French settee and
19th-century chairs
provide seating in the chinoiserie dining
room; the metal table
is a Martin Szekely design.

ABOVE

*Fabrics designed by Brandolini layer the walls and ceiling of
the master bath. A mirrored wainscot visually increases the size of the small space, and above it all
hangs a baroque-style shell chandelier made by Claire Cormier-Fauvel.*

OPPOSITE

*In the master bedroom, the bed is upholstered in 18th-century French fabric and dressed in linens
handmade in Vietnam. Framed gold-embroidered panels share the
wall with a painting by Philip Taaffe, a Van Day Truex drawing, and religious icons.*

THOMAS O'BRIEN

One day, after years of living decorously in his 1,100-square-foot apartment in New York, the designer Thomas O'Brien realized that, owing to his busy life—overseeing the eclectic SoHo shop Aero and creating home-furnishings and accessories lines for Hickory Chair, Safavieh, Groundworks, Target, and Reed & Barton, among others—he seldom saw more than the bedroom itself. In the meantime, the living room was evolving into a bric-a-brac limbo. "I was always cleaning it up," says O'Brien, who seems to collect just about anything that doesn't move, from figure drawings to blue jeans. "I didn't like to work or even entertain in there—the sofa was too low and too soft."

So the designer eventually decided to try something that many a six-year-old has dreamed of but that few grown-ups would dare: He moved the bed into the living room. O'Brien says transforming the bedroom into his study and the living room into sleeping quarters was exactly the right thing to do. "It's so wonderful to wake up in this great big space," he says. The inspiration prompted a full-fledged renovation, and only a handful of things made the cut, including the Russel Wright bed and an 18th-century carved cabinet. As for acquisitions, several pieces of the designer's Hickory Chair collection fit the bill, such as an angular secretary for the redesigned main room. In that same area, a graphic wool rug (O'Brien for Target) popped on a whitewashed hardwood floor, while wood storage boxes became a stand-in for a suite of closets. Added to that was a just-so assortment of ceramics, sculptures, and whatnot, and O'Brien had an interior chic enough to make anyone wonder: Why isn't my bed in the living room?

The makeover is a nod to the glamour of the artist's studio and to the interplay between creativity and domesticity. Specifically, O'Brien had the bohemian habitats of Mondrian and Brancusi in mind. "I had always loved images of those spaces," he says. "There's such great character to their openness." In the main room, O'Brien has waved off the properly hung picture and installed, with pushpins, an oversize bulletin board of inspiration where he posts whatever artist/textile/dog/dowager/architect/cowboy/ceramic/locale/what-have-you has caught his interest. It's all a reminder that living with style should mean being free to break away from symbolic boundaries, and still be able to keep old-fashioned concepts of elegance or clutter intact. When it comes right down to it, as long as you're not wearing your pajamas to work, who cares if you sleep in your living room? ■

PRECEDING PAGES
Interior designer Thomas O'Brien in the living room of his prewar Manhattan apartment; the space has 18-foot ceilings, whitewashed hardwood floors, original casement windows, and also functions as his bedroom.

ABOVE
A 4th-century Celtic bust is displayed on the pedestal; the Hallings secretary is from the designer's furniture collection for Hickory Chair.

RIGHT
A vintage Russel Wright bed and Shipwreck Rock by Ray Mortenson anchor a living room corner; O'Brien designed the bed linens.

OPPOSITE
An oversize bulletin board in the living room serves as a wall of inspiration. The folding library ladder is from Aero, his SoHo shop, and the Bennett storage boxes are a design for Hickory Chair.

MICHAEL S. SMITH

Michael S. Smith's house in Bel Air was simple in its first incarnation, a 1950s low-slung ranch that was reputedly built for a member of the Doheny oil dynasty. After a couple of walkabouts, however, the faded mid-20th-century charms that initially caught the designer's attention began to appear merely forlorn. "It had everything you could possibly want, but it was all in the wrong place," Smith explains.

Four years later, the little ranch house that could has been entirely obliterated from the eucalyptus-scented landscape through an inspired partnership with architect Oscar Shamamian. In its stead rises a sophisticated, slate-roofed brick house that would look right at home in a bucolic corner of Oxfordshire. "I am such an Anglophile," says the designer. "English houses are the prettiest, most comfortable houses in the world. Who are we kidding? Youthquakers are embracing tradition, and why not? It's the last meaningful thing."

Despite that extravagant PDA, the previous home Smith owned was fairly contemporary in tone. This time around, however, he and his partner, James Costos, an HBO executive, putter around comforting, high-ceilinged rooms that are chockablock with old-world touches: an antique Dutch folding screen, hemlock paneling, a billboard-size Peter Paul Rubens painting in a gilt-wood frame, canopy beds à la *Brideshead Revisited*.

"Fancy just creeps up on you," a smiling Smith says. In the master bedroom, a Sony flat-screen TV perches on a ducal-quality gilt-and-marble console, and in the poetically spare entrance hall, the fireplace is tended with a set of 1820s English tools, lovingly polished and ready for action. The beds are tumble-inviting jumbles of crisp linens by D. Porthault, cushions of Smith-designed chintz, and sprightly Moroccan and Indian fabrics.

"Some people think California is all guacamole and Eames furniture, but we have a big tradition of pretty houses, too," says the Orange County native. "One of my favorite things Joan Didion ever wrote was about California style, with its needlepoint rugs and potted orchids and Rigaud candles. That pretty much sums this place up."

Anglophile leanings aside, Smith hasn't forgotten his West Coast roots, which means loads of linen upholstery and not so much silk damask ("just a cushion or two," he insists). "Our place is *done*," Costos concedes. "But I find it casual, relaxed—not formal at all. It's filled with amazing things that Michael has found all over the world, yet the dogs jump on the sofas, and we're barefoot more often than not." ■

PRECEDING PAGES
*Interior designer Michael S. Smith at his home in
Bel Air, with Labradoodles Jasper and
Sport. The house was a collaboration between Smith and architect
Oscar Shamamian of
Ferguson & Shamamian Architects.*

OPPOSITE
*In the pattern-filled living room, eclectic
furnishings—including a Japanese low table and a 19th-
century English library chair—are arranged
beneath a Christine Taber painting. The sofa is upholstered in a
floral fabric from the Jasper collection by
Michael S. Smith, and the antique Tabriz carpet
is from Mansour.*

ABOVE
*De Gournay wallpaper hand-painted with
exotic birds perched in a Chinese-style
landscape brings the garden indoors. The dining chairs were
designed by Smith, the mahogany table
is a Regency antique, and the gilt-wood mirror dates
from the reign of George II.*

LEFT
The living room's Queen Anne–style
table expands for dinner parties, and O'Brien often seats
a guest on the bed.

ABOVE
The designer installed
a commercial-grade range by DCS in the kitchen; the
chrome-and-leather stool is vintage.

OPPOSITE
The desk, tubular chrome armchair,
and celestial chart in
the study are all vintage. The Miro lamp
is an O'Brien design for Visual
Comfort, and the floors
were finished with an industrial
high-gloss paint.

ABOVE
O'Brien removed a shelf
from his Sullivan bookcase by Hickory
Chair to fit a Sharp LCD
television; the chair and ottoman are also
his designs, and the
area rug is patchwork cowhide.

LEFT
A series of 1940s figure sketches
flanks the entrance to
the dressing room; the vintage Chinese table
holds an Opal Spiral
lamp designed for Target.

SIG BERGAMIN

"My house, just like me, isn't perfect."

The Brazilian architect Sig Bergamin is dimpled and darkly handsome, likes a party, and is a serious news junkie. But first and foremost, the man is a collector. All the usual stuff, of course: ceramics, paintings, glass. Even the structural materials of his home—located in a parklike island of repose in the center of São Paulo—are the result of inspired assemblage; the floors, staircase, and beams of the house were salvaged from an older place nearby. "You'd never know you were in the middle of the city," Bergamin says. "I wake up hearing birds every morning."

Additional bits of the decor have drifted in from considerably farther away, like wall and floor tiles that were picked up on one of his trips to Morocco; also from that North African kingdom is a luxurious and highly colorful array of tribal rugs and throws that come in handy on chilly evenings. Other collectibles were entirely unintentional. In the library, which is the site of relaxed, casual suppers—Sig's black Labrador retriever, Africa, pants happily under diners' feet, poised for any crumb that drops—there's a dressy Adam-style mantel that's, basically, a client reject. Yet amid Bergamin's thousand-volume cache of books on art, interiors, and travel, along with the occasional fat thriller, it's very much at home. From the lacquered languor of an antique Chinese canopy bed, guests can comfortably contemplate both shimmering 1960s Murano glass as well as an Andy Warhol dollar-sign painting. And in Bergamin's bedroom, a quietly luxe space free from the cacophony of furniture, magazines, friends, the nightly news, masses of McCoy pottery (have we mentioned that?), and clusters of photographs (forgot that, too), is displayed a tender letter written nearly 80 years ago by the Danish writer Isak Dinesen to the dashing English pilot she loved.

The real business of the house, however, takes place in the attic. Here, where muscular beams slice cool white walls and help rusticate blues and whites, can be found an office, a bar, a charming bathroom (with a dainty, Portuguese-tiled tub), and all the chairs, hassocks, sofas, and well-placed tables that conversation, cocktails, and communal news-channel watching might require. The many furnishings of this attic, as of the floors below, were retrieved from storage units spread across two hemispheres. Which means that Bergamin had to purchase only a few things for his residence, such as the dozens of Indian glass lanterns, hung in a manner that would never do for clients—naked bulbs on naked wires. "My house, just like me, isn't perfect," he says. ∎

PRECEDING PAGES
*The attic sitting room
of Sig Bergamin's São Paulo house is
furnished with a
striped-linen sofa swathed in an Indian
throw, and a collection
of antique Chinese porcelain.*

RIGHT
*Brazilian architect and interior designer
Sig Bergamin.*

BELOW
*In the library, Murano-glass vases
draped with beads
and an Andy Warhol painting; the curtains
are made from Moroccan tents.*

OPPOSITE
*The attic's crisp, cool scheme—
a dramatic beamed ceiling, denim-covered
upholstery, and casual
blue-and-white textiles—is designed to
distract visitors
from the Brazilian heat.*

ABOVE
A 19th-century Chinese
bed commands center stage in the living room;
Bergamin displays some of
his glass collection in the corner niche.

RIGHT
Moroccan tiles trim
the terrace's whirlpool with a kaleidoscope
of color.

OPPOSITE
The terrace's Victorian table
is set with porcelain from Vietnam, rustic rattan
chargers, and pressed-glass
goblets; the wall and floor tiles were found
in Morocco.

RIGHT
The walls of Bergamin's bedroom
are covered in coffee-brown
linen, the bedcover is from Provence, and
the totemlike wood
table lamps date from the 1940s.

BELOW
For a guest bathroom, Bergamin had
towels made to match the
bathtub's Portuguese tiles; the black-and-
white photos are by Tuca Reinés.

OPPOSITE
The distressed-wood ceiling
in a guest room was salvaged from a near
by 18th-century house.

ANTONY TODD

"You have to come up
with an idea and make it big."

For Antony Todd, the maestro behind many New York galas, first impressions are everything. "You have to come up with an idea and make it big," says Todd, whose eponymous company art-directs everything from parties to product design. "New Yorkers are spoiled by what they see every day, and their expectations are high, so it's really about the impact when people walk into a room. Somehow you have to transport them to a different place."

With his polished charm, movie-star looks, and jet-set elegance, this modern-day Cary Grant easily navigates the disparate worlds of society and Hollywood, art and fashion. His penchant for theatrical gestures—industrial-size elevators filled with giant pink cushions, Champagne, and cellists; glossy-white lofts packed with towering pyramids of bloodred roses; and couture-clad supermodels diving en masse off the side of a private yacht—is not surprising given a background studying set design in his native Australia.

Todd's apartment, which occupies two floors of a Victorian townhouse, has a similar degree of visual and tactile appeal. "I wanted the rooms to feel personal and lived in," the designer explains, "but also young and underdone, rather than too fussy and formal." The result, which was whipped up in only three weeks, has a relaxed sophistication: a nonchalant melding of traditional and contemporary, formal and casual, high- and low-end, new and antique. It's a harmonious mishmash of English, French, Italian, Asian, early-American, and custom-made furnishings, many of them crafted to Todd's specifications, that all share a certain honesty of form.

The parlor-floor entrance—tall French doors open onto a large reception area that doubles as the dining room—is all understated drama. A ten-foot round oak table serves as the monumental centerpiece and social anchor to the apartment. "I've had cocktail parties where everyone gathers around this table and all the other rooms are empty." Flanking the fireplace are neoclassical-style consoles and mirrors made from the panels of antique folding screen. Todd likens the parlor floor to a "thoroughfare of rooms"—one side of the reception area leads to the living room, the other to a sunroom that overlooks the garden. Downstairs he has carved out a Zenlike master bedroom suite.

Like any good art director, he employs a lot of white space. "You can read the objects," Todd says. "They have room to breathe. But hopefully it's not too austere. I want it to feel warm and inviting at the same time." ■

INSIDE INFORMATION

■ My favorite objects have simple, clean lines and are from different periods. And I like to pair classic and modern pieces with something unexpected, like really romantic, over-the-top flowers.

■ When starting to design an interior, think carefully about the floor plan and visualize how you would truly like to live in the space—not only when you're home alone but also when the rooms are filled with guests for a party.

■ I like to play with scale, really mix it up. Powerful, gutsy design statements need space to breathe. A dramatic color palette or large-scale furnishings make a strong impact, but even small accessories—especially eccentric, exotic ones—can add personality and balance.

PRECEDING PAGES
Antony Todd in the living room of his
Greenwich Village duplex.

TOP LEFT
In the living room, chocolate-color
mohair was used to upholster
a 1940s bergère and an armless sofa that Todd
designed for the space.

BOTTOM LEFT
Curtains of fine wool hang from
a ceiling-mounted framework over Todd's bed;
the blanket is by Hermès,
and the floor is carpeted with sea-
grass matting.

ABOVE
A silver-gelatin print by Bill Phelps
hangs above the
desk in Todd's home office.

OPPOSITE
Art by David Carino dominates the
sunroom; the settee, pedestal
table, horn side table, and rug all date
from the 1800s.

JAOUAD KADIRI

*"It's not about one particular place. It's about
every place we've been."*

Northwest of the city of Marrakech grows the Palmeraie, a peaceful and fabled oasis of wild palm trees that sprawls for miles beneath the snowcapped High Atlas Mountains. This frond-befringed paradise is also the area's most desirable neighborhood, and here amid the mega-size pleasure domes, businessman Jaouad Kadiri has settled in a country house whose wall-to-wall blush puts a decidedly North African spin on the phrase *think pink*.

Flame-tinted bougainvillea clamber up the red-clay ramparts. Fuchsia canopies flutter on the roof terrace, and silk cushions the color of strawberries beckon from every banquette. Out back, beyond an open-air pavilion pierced with windows in the shape of Arabic scent bottles, awaits a sumptuous daybed shaded by rosy sequined parasols. "Pink is a very happy color," says Kadiri, a nightclub impresario–turned–hotel developer who created this magical abode in collaboration with Stuart Church, an architect based in Tangier. "And I wanted a happy house."

La maison Kadiri has strong regional underpinnings (a fortresslike silhouette, classic adobe walls), but exotic details give it a mix-master fizz. Windows are eccentrically modeled to resemble pendant blossoms or elongated decanters. The Moorish-looking mosaics are actually Uzbek in origin and are executed in modish shades of jade and aquamarine. The exaggerated, scalloped arches that link the rooms were inspired by the palaces of Gujarat. And instead of the central courtyard typical of Moroccan architecture, Kadiri's four-bedroom house is arranged around a 27-foot-square living room, whose painted cedar ceiling rises to a breathtaking 30 feet.

"It's not about one particular place," Kadiri says, explaining the building's Orientalist atmosphere. "It's about every place we've been." Trips to India yielded bolts of sari fabric to drape the canopy beds, 17th-century Portuguese Colonial candlesticks, and processional parasols fit for a maharajah. Berber carpets soften the cool, polished floors, and strands of fat cinnabar-color beads from the Marrakech souks lie coiled in silver bowls.

A broad-minded attitude guided the development of the gardens as well. The original olive grove has been lovingly preserved, but its dusty-green foliage is now enriched with global flora: cow's-foot orchid trees (*Bauhinia congesta*) from India; Washingtonia palms from the royal palace in Marrakech; ten varieties of eucalyptus; a Himalayan flowering vine known as beauty of the night; and scores of roses—yes, all of them pink. ∎

PRECEDING PAGES
Uzbek-inspired tilework backs
a banquette in the
three-story living room of Jaouad Kadiri's
house; the English-style
armchairs are upholstered in old
Persian rugs.

OPPOSITE
Berber rugs and silk cushions
made from saris brighten a banquette
in the pool pavilion.

ABOVE
Shaded by Washingtonia
palms, the pool pavilion is built of lime,
soil, and cement and
trimmed with handmade bricks.

LEFT
Indian palace
architecture inspired the dramatic
scalloped arches
that link the house's rooms
and corridors.

149

ABOVE
Pastel cottons and silk veils drape a guest chamber known as
the Jade Room. The Venetian-style mirror was designed by Stuart Church and made by craftsmen in Tangier.

OPPOSITE
Trips to India yielded embroidered and spangled
pink and red saris to decorate Kadiri's canopy bed. The Gothic-style mirrored side table is
a Stuart Church design.

MICHAEL LEVA

"I bought what I liked.
I knew eventually I'd be able to bring it all together someplace.
And that place turned out to be here."

For some, buying a weekend house is a question of love at first sight. For others, it is a rational process of compiling a list of needs and making a decisive choice. Then there are home buyers like fashion designer/interior decorator/author Michael Leva, for whom the search involves only torture and regret. He almost closed on a grand Dutch Colonial in New Jersey before discovering that it had an illegal cesspool. A gracious place in Dutchess County, New York, that was almost his turned out to be infested with termites. As for the best Georgian house on the Hudson River, it was next to a cement factory (cue dust and noise).

Eventually, however, Leva came across a 1765 saltbox in Litchfield County, Connecticut, and bought it. The ceilings weren't as high as he craved, and though the house had been renovated in the 1980s, its previous owners had saved as much of the original structure as possible. "There was something modern, almost minimal about it," Leva says. "The colors of the granite fireplace began to inspire me." Not that the process was easy. "One day I had five cans in front of me, all different pale grays, almost whites, and I realized that if I just painted everything in those five shades, the place would actually work. Then I could move in my furniture."

And he certainly had enough, from a Gustavian settee to a "1920s Louis repro" love seat and a bed that Leva purchased in his 20s and assembled and painted himself. "Every time I finish a job, I buy an important piece," he says. "I've always convinced myself that it helps me get my next job." Whatever didn't fit into his small Manhattan rentals he put into storage. "I bought what I liked," Leva acknowledges. "I knew eventually I'd be able to bring it all together someplace. And that place turned out to be here." Among his perfect finds were two low, sleek 1970s sofas on chrome legs that were designed by the father of noted photographer Philip-Lorca diCorcia. Leva even found a spot for the crystal chandelier he had bought to hang from a high ceiling in that New Jersey Dutch Colonial.

But in this story of despair followed by redemption—the luminous and serene rooms, the welcoming kitchen, the lush perennial beds, the sweet peas climbing trellises by the pool—what's most surprising is that it all occurred within two short years. "If you have an aesthetic, a consistent point of view," says Leva, "I guess that carries you through." Even to the extent that you can discover beauty in the most unexpected of places. ■

PRECEDING PAGES
*Designer Michael Leva's charming 1765
saltbox in Litchfield County,
Connecticut, which he filled with an elegant mix of
top-notch modern furnishings
and Swedish and French antiques.*

OPPOSITE
*Vintage Venetian and American
glass in the kitchen; the
cabinetry is by Stephen Piscuskas of York
Street Studio, the refrigerator
is by Sub-Zero, and the
mercury-glass pendant shades
are antique.*

ABOVE
*A 1970s sofa in the living room
is upholstered in mohair by Clarence House;
the table lamp is made of an
early-20th-century pharmacy bottle
filled with colored water.*

LEFT
*The dining room features a
Venetian-style table and late-1800s French
convex mirrors.*

ABOVE
Leva found the library's Gustavian settee and the 1930s velvet-covered stools at a flea market in Paris.

RIGHT
In a guest room, vintage framed butterflies and a 1950s Dutch klismos chair.

OPPOSITE
Leva's bedroom is furnished with a Louis-Philippe chair, Directoire mirror, cobalt-blue glass lantern, and a Shaker-style four-poster.

SHEILA BRIDGES

"I don't like things to be matchy-matchy.
Real life is having different experiences and relationships, with
furniture as well as people."

There are many things to obsess over in Sheila Bridges's apartment. There's the size: deluxe, complete with three bedrooms, formal living and dining rooms, and maid's quarters. There's the location: the top floor of a landmark 1901 Clinton & Russell building in central Harlem, just a few blocks north of Central Park. There's the symphony of rich colors. And there are the scores of lighthearted yet elegant objects and furnishings. But perhaps the most seductive bit of the interior designer's handiwork is one appreciated not through your eyes but via the soles of your feet.

Bridges starts her magic carpet ride at the front door, when she offers you a pair of Moroccan slippers. "It's not so much about the idea that the city is filthy, or ruining anything precious," she says. "I just want people to feel at ease. I am always in bare feet." Going shoeless is, of course, a surefire way to feel at ease. But the apartment, which has been totally redone in the past few years, is as globe-trotting as it is down-home. The romp begins immediately, in the tangerine blast of an entry, where the focal point is a *borne d'hôtel* reminiscent of fin de siècle Paris. Off this a smorgasbord of doorways opens. There is the blue-toned living room, anchored by the playful round shapes of a Swedish grandfather clock and an antique convex mirror. The bold orange, black, and gray stripes and exotic furnishings of the home office cum guest room conjure a Victorian explorer's London flat or a 1970s Pop interior, depending on how you look at it. As for the apple-green dining room, it is outfitted with an assortment of curious chairs, back-to-back demilune tables, and a Venetian-glass chandelier.

"I don't like things to be matchy-matchy," says Bridges. "Real life is having different experiences and relationships, with furniture as well as people." Which explains why her apartment combines elements of 19th-century Paris, the Harlem Renaissance, and 1950s New York, three eras that have captured her heart. This scope is illustrated nowhere more concretely than in the library. Through a painstaking process that involved both a signmaker and a decorative painter, Bridges applied passages and quotations from her favorite writers to the walls, everyone from Langston Hughes to Emily Dickinson to Dr. Seuss. One, from Zora Neale Hurston, seems particularly appropriate: "Here was peace. She pulled in her horizon like a great fish-net. Pulled it from around the waist of the world and draped it over her shoulder. So much of life in its meshes!" And here, too, so much of it meshes. ■

PRECEDING PAGES
The living room of Sheila Bridges's
apartment, which is located
in a landmark Harlem building, features
soothing colors and a
graceful mix of antique furnishings.

LEFT
The living room's grandfather clock
is from Evergreen Antiques,
the cocktail table is vintage T. H. Robsjohn-
Gibbings, the curtains are made
of a Nancy Corzine botanical print, and
the rug is by Odegard. North
Parterre, Versailles, a photograph
by Kelly Grider, is
displayed above the antique settee.

ABOVE
Bridges furnished the dining
room with a pair of
demilunes and a suite of antique French
Louis XVI–style side chairs.

RIGHT
Interior designer Sheila Bridges.

ABOVE
In the office/guest room, a Korean
blanket chest and an
antique neoclassical chair; a Moroccan rug
covers the bed, and the
striped wall treatment was created
by Pintura Studios.

RIGHT
A borne d'hôtel in the entrance hall,
which is painted deep
orange; a selection of Moroccan slippers
awaits guests.

OPPOSITE
A series of hand-painted engravings
hangs above an antique
desk purchased at auction; the chair, a Bridges
design, is upholstered
in a Timney Fowler fabric.

INSIDE INFORMATION

■ Soothing colors are great in rooms you use all the time. The blue in my living room is fairly bold, but it's ethereal and relaxing, too. That's a feeling you want most of the time.

■ Spaces where you don't necessarily spend a tremendous amount of time —entrance halls, bathrooms, libraries—are where you can take big color risks. An entrance hall can be bright orange, like mine, because you're only walking through it, not hanging out there. The same with home offices, where you don't spend the whole day. Mine has bold orange, gray, and black stripes, which helps keep me alert and invigorated.

■ The way to make these differences in color work is to tie the spaces together by painting the trim the same throughout. That's how you make the rooms seem unified rather than schizophrenic.

TOP LEFT
Some of Bridges's favorite
quotations, hand-painted by Pintura Studios,
cover the walls of the library.

ABOVE
Bridges upholstered an antique side chair
in a subtle silk stripe.

LEFT
The chest in the master
bedroom is Gustavian, and the antique French
musician's chair was
found in Charlottesville, Virginia.

OPPOSITE
The damask-pattern walls were hand-painted;
the headboard is covered in
a Brunschwig & Fils silk, and the bed linens
are by Frette.

ART

& CULTURE

CANDACE BUSHNELL

*"I love crystal chandeliers
and gold leaf, velvets and mirrors—things that are old and
glittery, that come with past lives."*

I'm the kind of person who would have liked to have lived at the Plaza. I love crystal chandeliers and gold leaf, velvets and mirrors—things that are old and glittery, that come with past lives. So the moment my husband and I first walked into our home, we knew that this was the place.

Built in the 1920s, reputedly as bachelor pads for young men making their fortunes on Wall Street, the Greenwich Village building's apartments have sunken living rooms and wood-burning fireplaces (some even have Juliet balconies from which, I imagine, the bachelors could yell down to their friends on the street). Back in the '20s, the place was considered to have every modern convenience. By the time my ballet-dancer husband, Charles Askegard, and I moved in, 80 years later, it was a wreck. The closets had been ripped out, the kitchen had no cabinets, and the dining room contained strange built-ins. "I just know you'll be able to turn this into a tiny jewel," the real-estate agent gushed. I smiled gamely, then called my good friend Susan Forristal, a former top model–turned–interior designer, who calmly put together a renovation team and served as the project manager.

The first step was to restore the elements of the apartment that had been taken out and then to rejigger the layout of the bathroom, bedroom, and dining room to allow for closets. I am very happy to say that, despite lacking any skill in geometry, I was the one who figured out how to enlarge the bathroom. It was a moment of such eureka proportions that I still think of it from time to time with enormous pleasure. As for the living room, I thought, why not turn it into a ballroom, with a black-and-white checkerboard floor, some chandeliers, and very little else? A good decorator never tells her client that a certain idea is insane. Instead of pointing out that a ballroom isn't appropriate in a 1,200-square-foot apartment, Susan merely priced out the cost of replacing the floor—something in the neighborhood of $50,000—which put my misguided decorating ideas firmly to rest.

One rule of decorating is that you're supposed to start with a rug, but we did things differently. Among the first pieces Susan found for us were golden sconces and a palm-leaf lamp, followed by 1920s mirrored side tables. Then we chose a minty green velvet for the Louis XV sofa we bought from the novelist Jay McInerney. The living room looks fairly formal, but hidden in a cabinet under the bookshelves is a bar and mini fridge, usually stocked with Champagne. It may not be the Plaza, but when it comes to fun, we give those bachelors a run for their money. ■

PRECEDING PAGES
In the living room of Candace Bushnell's
Manhattan apartment, Caio
Fonseca's Fifth Street Painting C04.13 overlooks a
19th-century tufted bustle chair, Moroccan
poufs from John Derian, and an
Oushak rug. Bushnell and her husband, Charles
Askegard, purchased the Louis XV
sofa from a friend, writer Jay McInerney.

OPPOSITE
A hot-pink, 19th-century Venetian chaise
longue adds a dose of drama
to a corner of the living room; the vintage gold-
leafed sheaf sconce is one
of a pair flanking the mantel, which is
original to the apartment.

RIGHT
Novelist Candace Bushnell.

BELOW
The kitchen features wood-and-glass
cabinetry and soapstone counters; the porcelain-
enamel light fixture is a vintage find.

OPPOSITE
Bushnell collaborated with decorator Susan
Forristal on the interior design of
the apartment. The den is furnished with ebonized campaign
chairs with white cowhide seats,
a velvet-upholstered sofa, and a rug by Madeline
Weinrib from ABC Carpet & Home.

ABOVE
Bushnell's bed is dressed with a vintage
embroidered bedcover and
an antique suzani; the table lamps are a midcentury
design, and the painting,
Dutchman's Dawn II, *is by Ellen Kozak.*

LEFT
Forristal reproduced a
poster of Bushnell onto wallpaper that lines the
walls of the powder room.

BEN STILLER &
CHRISTINE TAYLOR

*"It's a commitment to live with a particular style,
but if you can update it to make it functional and still maintain the integrity
of the house, it's a great combo."*

Once upon a time American movie stars lived in Spanish Revival houses and were attended to by uniformed chauffeurs and maids in frilly aprons. Ben Stiller and Christine Taylor don't have hot-and-cold running staff, but the actors and their two young children do live in Andalusian splendor. What started out as a modest 1920s stucco hacienda in the Hollywood Hills has been transformed into a rambling flamenco-hip home whose dark beams and Iberian ironwork give it Oscar-worthy depth. However there's a difference. Instead of ubiquitous Malibu tile, the house incorporates a shimmering take on Moroccan *zellige*. Inquisition-style iron chandeliers were eschewed in favor of lighter Scandinavian models. And since Stiller and Taylor had no intention of sitting on carved furniture fit for a conquistador, designers Robin Standefer and Stephen Alesch trucked in Dunbar-style sofas, along with vintage vases and a bronze-and-leather library ladder that looks like it might have been wrought by Pierre Chareau.

"It's a commitment to live with a particular style," says Taylor, "but if you can update it to make it functional and still maintain the integrity of the house, it's a great combo." The foursome pored over books about Spanish architecture and its Moorish influences and took field trips around the neighborhood. "Function came first, and design details came second, though a very close second," the actress explains. The plumbing is modern but the look is timeworn; the garage doors are made from battered 300-year-old wood; and the cabinets in the gleaming white kitchen are supported by hand-turned spindles inspired by those spotted in an old bakery.

The heart of Taylor and Stiller's house is the family room, adjacent to the kitchen. "Every family nests in a home differently, but everybody hangs out in the kitchen," says Stiller. "It's just a universal law of nature, like gravity or aging." The designers also created a combination library and kids' room, with blackboards set into the cabinets so the children can draw to their hearts' content, and topping the cabinetry is a hand-painted frieze of stars and planets.

So what's here for adults? A jungly garden, for one thing, conceived by landscape architect Mark Bartos and shaded with massive trees. There's an outdoor fireplace for kicking back on cool summer nights. A terrace is party-ready with a massive wood dining table, and in the master suite, there's an enormous white bathtub for soaking away postshoot tensions. Some movie-star requirements never change. ■

PRECEDING PAGES
The terrace of Ben Stiller and
Christine Taylor's house,
which was designed by Robin Standefer and
Stephen Alesch of Roman and
Williams, features
Mission-influenced furniture and a
Moroccan light.

LEFT
Custom-made button-tufted
sofas furnish the living
room; the iron chandelier is a flea-
market discovery.

OPPOSITE
In the living room, a selection from
the couple's photography
collection is on display, including images by
Matthew Barney
and Hiroshi Sugimoto.

RIGHT
A vintage Poul Henningsen chandelier
and Belgian advertising
poster add a funky touch to the atrium;
the armchair and
cabinet are by Christian Liaigre.

BELOW
The pool area has a Mediterranean-
meets–Middle East attitude,
thanks to star-shape tiles and a Moroccan-
style mosaic fountain.

ABOVE
The master bath features a tub
from the Water Monopoly, and Pier sconces and
an antique metal medical
cabinet from Urban Archaeology; the tub filler
is by Lefroy Brooks.

RIGHT
The high-ceilinged kitchen features
custom-made glossy white
cabinetry, a deep Kallista sink, and vintage
chairs from Wyeth.

OPPOSITE
Standefer and Alesch designed the
family room's cabinetry
with an inset blackboard and a hand-painted frieze
of stars and planets.

LYNN DE ROTHSCHILD

The family name is legendary. The building is one of the most sought after in Manhattan. So when Lynn Forester, shortly before she married the British banker Sir Evelyn de Rothschild in 2000, bought a duplex in River House, a 1931 landmark on the East River, it was no ordinary real-estate transaction: She was grappling with history. Still, it was pretty clear who would retain the upper hand, for few women are as modern-minded as Lady de Rothschild. The mother of two grown sons from her marriage to Andrew Stein, the former New York City Council president, she was one of the first to understand the implications of cellular and broadband technology and made fortunes off both. Now she has joined a family renowned for its opulent sense of decoration. "I respect *le style Rothschild*," she says, "but that wasn't the way I wanted to live." As Michael S. Smith, the interior designer who took the duplex into his expert hands, explains, "Lynn loves to take off her shoes and put her feet up."

Today the walls of the living room, once covered in vivid yellow damask, are pale gray Venetian plaster, a serene backdrop for its understated composition of cream, silver, and celadon with glints of gilt and glass. Nothing detracts from the killer river views or the museum-quality art and furniture. The stools are by Diego Giacometti, and the nesting tables are by Ruhlmann. An early Jackson Pollock hangs above a 17th-century chest in the entrance hall. It's all pretty impressive, but the apartment is comfortably stylish. The sofas and chairs certainly aren't overstuffed, but they have as much down as possible without subverting their clean lines. Silk rugs, soft carpets, and cool marble floors (not to mention tiles of dark-green leather paving the family room) make the spaces as enticing for bare feet as for ball gowns. Stacks of books are everywhere. The sunny kitchen is, however, pristine—purposefully so. "I cook not at all," Rothschild says. "For Mother's Day one year, the students had to bring in their mother's favorite recipe. My son claimed mine was 'Burnt.'" Knockout glamour is reserved for upstairs, principally the master bedroom, which is anchored by a spectacular shagreen bed whose curves sweep like a scallop shell's.

These days Sir Evelyn and his wife can often be found in London, where they live in the former studio of the artist John Singer Sargent. But Rothschild insists she's a true-blue New Yorker. "I don't spend as much time in the apartment as I might like, but I love being here," she says. Smith understands her feelings exactly. "It's not about topiaries or Staffordshire bull terriers. It's deeply personal, and after all, isn't that what the Rothschild style is known for?" ∎

PRECEDING PAGES
Lynn Forester de Rothschild in the sitting room
of the Manhattan duplex she
shares with her husband, Sir Evelyn de Rothschild;
Michael S. Smith designed the interior.

ABOVE
Black/White, a 1988 oil on canvas
by Ellsworth Kelly,
dominates the living room; the sofa, by Jonas
Upholstery, is covered in
a Claremont gauffrage damask.

RIGHT
A late-17th-century bronze-inlaid chest and
a pair of 1930s French oak stools
in the entrance hall; Jackson Pollock's Composition
with Sgraffito is
displayed above the chest.

OPPOSITE
In the living room, Achrome, a kaolin
on canvas by Piero Manzoni,
hangs above an 18th-century marble chimneypiece
from Chesney's; the
iron stool is by Diego Giacometti.

ABOVE
The dining room's 18th-century
Chinese wallpaper was
purchased at auction; the antique mahogany
table is from Christopher Hodsoll,
and the George I–style
gilt-wood chairs are upholstered
in moss-green silk
velvet from the Silk Trading Co.

RIGHT
Smith designed the kitchen's
oak-and-steel barstools;
the range is by Viking, and the pot rack was
custom made.

OPPOSITE
The designer created a luxe
wood-paneled library; the sofa is covered in
a Lelièvre fabric.

ABOVE
The master bedroom features a dramatic bed sheathed in shagreen;
the curtains are made of a Bennison floral damask, and the walls are covered in silk from Michael S. Smith's
fabric collection for Cowtan & Tout.

OPPOSITE
The master bath's whirlpool tub and hand shower are by Michael S. Smith for Kallista;
the Jules Leleu chair is from Maison Gerard.

DAVID SALLE

*"The house is
very much a self-portrait."*

The artist David Salle has made a career of creating provocative wholes from disparate elements—small canvases inset within larger ones, grisaille images painted over colored ones, abstract elements jostling figures, romantic visions of the past colliding with the brutal present—and he's done nothing less in his Brooklyn house. Indeed, it seems fitting that a man who has achieved fame with his layering of images should find himself in a home/studio that is a cheek-by-jowl clash of a gracious pre–Civil War townhouse and a building that was once a Masonic lodge.

"They had been abandoned years before, even by the squatters," he says. "The roof was open to the sky. It was too big for most individuals but too small for a developer." With its corner location and three exposures, however, the 10,000-square-foot space was ideal for an artist who wanted a vast studio for his oversize canvases and enough room left over so he could live on a scale that expands the domestic ideal without distorting it.

The layout largely dictated the use of the rooms—an expansive studio that runs the length of the first floor; the kitchen, library, and double-height living and dining areas on the second floor; the master bedroom suite on the third; and an office/sitting room on the fourth—but there were two major problems. There was no outdoor space, and the rooms upstairs were, architect Christian Hubert recalls, "dark and nasty." To remedy both, the architect cut away part of the brick building to make a terrace, and for the townhouse he designed a three-story extension under a zinc-covered roof that curves down to form an exterior wall. That gave the upper floors more windows and provided the spacious master bedroom with a terrace and a garden. Even the master bath has a terrace.

Throughout the house are exquisite yet unconventional details—the surprise of a Francesco Clemente drawing against a decorative Dagobert Peche wallpaper, a wall covered with industrial felt in the library. In the baths, the woodwork evokes Japan; in the bedroom, high Italian Modernism. The library makes subtle allusions to Arts and Crafts simplicity, and the kitchen and dining area's use of limed oak recalls French '40s style. "David's aesthetic is about juxtapositions, and I wanted to make an architectural analog to that," says Hubert. "And because he was so involved, the house is very much a self-portrait." Adds Salle, "I was a little concerned about how the neighborhood would react, but people stop me on the street all the time to tell me how much they like it." ∎

PRECEDING PAGES
*The artist David Salle at his
Brooklyn, New York, studio, seated in front of
one of his paintings.*

LEFT
*Architect Christian Hubert melded a
pre–Civil War townhouse
and a corniced brick building that once served
as a Masonic lodge into
a sprawling modern residence.*

BELOW
*Works in Salle's studio
include* Flamenco, *in the foreground, and*
Funny Face, *against
the far wall; the armchairs are
vintage Danish.*

OPPOSITE
*Winnie, the artist's vizsla, relaxes
on a Florence Knoll
armchair. The wing chairs were designed by
Italian architect Gio Ponti.*

OPPOSITE
The pale, shipshape kitchen
has a glass-mosaic backsplash by Bisazza,
a range and hood by Wolf,
and open shelving. The cabinets are
of European white oak.

ABOVE
The Scandinavian-spare living
room features a Florence Knoll sofa and
Kaare Klint armchairs;
Salle's Girl Reading hangs above the Hubert-
designed fireplace surround.

LEFT
The breakfast area is furnished with
limed-oak benches and
a late-1940s Finnish school chair; the Teardrop
light is from Tucker Robbins.

OPPOSITE
*A painting by Alex Katz hangs above
the headboard in the
master bedroom; the bedcover is from India, and
Marco Zanuso's Martingala
armchairs flank the Saarinen side table.*

ABOVE
*A 1950s Donald Knorr
metal chair is paired with an early-20th-century
Navajo rug in the sitting room.*

LEFT
*The library was designed in
homage to the American Arts and Crafts period.
Vintage photographs
are propped on the bookcase ledge.*

CINDY CRAWFORD

*"When you live on the beach,
you use it; we feel like we're on a perpetual vacation."*

"When you live on the beach, you use it," says Cindy Crawford, the supermodel with the sultry-but-wholesome looks. "We feel like we're on a perpetual vacation," she continues. "Our kids are in the pool five times a week. We live outdoors as much as in, and it's always casual—we are a no-coaster household."

The home that she shares with her husband, bar impresario/real-estate developer Rande Gerber, and their young children, Kaia and Presley, is perched on a precipice overlooking the Pacific in Malibu, and though the property, which slopes down to a private beach, is grand even by Hollywood standards, the house—the result of five years of planning, building, and decorating—exudes warmth and welcome. "We wanted to live like we were at a resort," Crawford says. "So we tried to think of everything we love about our beach vacations."

The family's life is focused on the outdoors, and so is the house. The principal rooms have pocket doors that remain open, weather permitting, leading to ample decks and an infinity pool. Yet the couple came to the project with very different ideas: He hates the Oriental rugs she loves, and she prefers a cozier look to his edgy, modernist leanings. Enter interior designer Michael S. Smith and architect Oscar Shamamian, who came up with a house that Crawford characterizes as resembling "a sugar plantation in the tropics"—part Colonial (classic proportions, clean lines), part Caribbean (indoor-outdoor living, tropical materials). To convey spareness and simplicity while keeping the spirit earthy yet romantic, Smith limited patterns, choose quality pieces versus "fancy stuff," and allowed architectural details their own voice. In the living room, for example, the recessed squares in the stone around the fireplace add an elegant element, as do shuttered doors in the bar and carved moldings in the master bath. A white-gold–leaf ceiling in the dining room and classic bamboo shades in nearly every window let light play capriciously.

"It may seem like a one-note idea of wood-and-white," Smith says, "but it's not. It's complex and sophisticated." Fabrics have subtle, engaging textures that animate the rooms without making a big deal about it. Venetian-plaster walls add a quiet background sheen. An assortment of Moroccan wool rugs convey a sense of exotic history but are tough enough to be beach-appropriate. And curtains can transform a sunny room into a virtual tent.

"The house is bigger than the sum of its parts," concludes Smith. "We all nudged, pushed, fought, and inspired each other," says Crawford of the collaboration. "And the house is so much better for our family because of it." ■

INSIDE INFORMATION

▪ This is the first place we've done together; this is our married house. Rande is edgy and Armani-esque—he loves the look of the Amanresorts—and I prefer rooms that are cozy. We each had to step out of our safety zones and find something we both liked.

▪ To enter our house from the front courtyard, guests cross over a small reflecting pool; there's actually a little bridge to the front door. As soon it opens, you can see straight through the house to the sea and sky beyond. We had our home feng shui'd, and it turned out that the good that came in flowed right out the other side, so we placed a large round table in the center of the hall.

▪ When Rande and I have friends over for dinner, we start with drinks around the fire pit on the deck, and if it's warm enough, we eat outside. If not, we move to the dining room. But we always end up out by the fire.

PRECEDING PAGES
Cindy Crawford in the family room
of the Malibu home she
shares with her husband, Rande Gerber, and
their two young children. Interior
designer Michael S. Smith and architect
Oscar Shamamian
collaborated on the project.

OPPOSITE
Custom-made teak sofas and a
pair of Charles Jacobsen
cocktail tables in the living room; an
iconic black-and-white
photo of Crawford by Herb Ritts is
displayed on the mantel.

TOP RIGHT
Reproduction armchairs by
Michael S. Smith
are used in the dining room; the ceiling
is papered in gleaming squares
of white-gold leaf, and the
multimedia work, Scholars Rocks, *is*
by Nancy Lorenz.

CENTER RIGHT
The main house and a
series of terraces are built into the cliffs
overlooking the sea.

BOTTOM RIGHT
The cabana is furnished with comfortable
rattan armchairs and a
19th-century Chinese lantern.

ABOVE
Resembling a room on a 1920s
yacht, the master bath
is paneled in dark, polished wood; the
bath and sink fittings are
by Michael S. Smith for Kallista.

RIGHT
A Peter Beard photograph fills a wall
of the sitting room.

OPPOSITE
Midcentury Beni Ouarain rugs
from Morocco add a
plush touch to the master bedroom; the
windows are curtained with
linen panels, and the
bed linens are by Nancy Koltes.

JOHN DERIAN

*"I love that wrecked,
ruined, and decaying look."*

The decoupage artist John Derian has been hitting flea markets since he was a teenager, initially with his sister and then with an eccentric aunt. And some of his best collegiate memories are of cutting class to scour thrifts and fleas on Boston's North Shore with his first boyfriend. A career of truancy doesn't usually pay off, but for Derian, who now lives in New York, it has proven not to be the worst course of study. His whimsical decoupage plates, lamps, and paperweights, all featuring various lovely and/or witty 19th-century ephemera and artwork, are increasingly sought after by people who have become weary of floor-to-rafters modernism. And his gem of an apartment is a demonstration of how slow and steady not only wins the race but looks pretty good doing it.

Derian's one-bedroom pad on the Lower East Side boasts not a single designer object; even the stove is antique. "I'm not sure if it's safe to use the oven," he admits. The well-worn modern chairs around the dining table? Derian doesn't know who designed them. In the dining room, a rustic and narrow X-base table sits squarely atop two Oriental carpets. A small crystal chandelier and a paper lantern (minus the paper) hang overhead. Three handsome shelves made of massive antique floorboards hold the old art books and magazines he leafs through for inspiration. A supermodel-thin antique cupboard is full of rocks, shells, crystals, and whatnot. Old amber beads, a find in Marrakech, hang on its latch. Nearby, what looks like either a nasty mass of twigs or a very expensive artwork is in fact an arrangement of dried vines by his friend Christopher Bassett.

John Derian has an eye, that's for sure—a mirror eaten away by time; a pink photograph by Jack Pierson; a tray of broken sticks of sealing wax (who knew it was so hard and brittle?). If some of today's interiors feel like nautilus shells, crafted with a precision and purity, Derian's place feels as though it were lovingly assembled by a highly evolved but not terribly orderly squirrel. It's an effect enhanced by the fact that, as cracks have appeared in the plaster over the years, Derian has merely patched them, but not repainted. "I love that wrecked, ruined, and decaying look," he says. One only has to look at the wing chair in the living room, whose fringy upholstery has been so finely shredded one would think it had been produced by the workroom of a Paris couturier. In fact, it was done by his cat. You can't buy that kind of handiwork. ∎

PRECEDING PAGES
The living room of John Derian's
apartment on Manhattan's
Lower East Side features an idiosyncratic
assemblage of offbeat
collections and humble furnishings.

LEFT
Decoupage artist and shop owner
John Derian outside
his store, which is located a few blocks from
his apartment.

BELOW
Derian, who has shopped flea
markets since he was a teenager, uses a
vintage boat fender
as an ottoman in his living room.

OPPOSITE
An 1860s American cupboard
in the dining room
holds organic treasures and pieces of
mercury glass.

OPPOSITE
The dining table is American, circa
1820, and the decoupage
Spider Web platter is a Derian design; the
shelves were made
from antique floorboards.

ABOVE
Derian's antique iron bed is
dressed with a mix
of new and vintage bedding; the sea sponge
was a gift from his sister,
and the curtain in the foreground
is made of
French 1930s floral fabric.

LEFT
Derian's cat, Skip, in the kitchen;
the lamp was found
at the Clignancourt flea market in
Paris, and the
animal cutouts are vintage.

SARAH JESSICA PARKER

*"We didn't want anything stuffy or showy;
we wanted color and light, and comfort, comfort, comfort."*

When Eric Hughes, a Hollywood executive–turned–interior decorator, began designing a weekend house in Bridge-hampton, New York, for actress Sarah Jessica Parker, he knew it had to be a place that could handle sandy feet, damp bathing suits, and lots of people. Within biking distance of the beach, the house is one of the few places where Parker and her husband, Matthew Broderick, can decompress with their young son, James Wilkie.

"We didn't want anything stuffy or showy," says the actress, best known for her star turn on *Sex and the City*. "We wanted color and light, and comfort, comfort, comfort," where they can play Ping-Pong and entertain. For years, real-estate agents offered places that were too fancy and lacked local character. Then Parker found a 19th-century farmhouse flooded with natural light and graced with high ceilings. The first step was to add an expansive wraparound porch that could accommodate groupings of stylish black wicker furniture and up to 20 people for meals. Inside, Hughes widened the doorways, opened up the living spaces to give the house better flow, and painted all the walls with Benjamin Moore's Super White. "I wanted to let the architecture speak for itself," he explains, "and then fill the rooms with punches of color." At Parker's request, the kitchen cabinetry is a glossy tulip-red.

The decoration is inspired by one of Hughes's idols, Billy Baldwin, a design star of the 1960s. A classic sofa is upholstered in the legend's favorite brown denim, and his iconic spatter print shows up on a window seat. In the master bedroom is a linen-covered Karl Springer console, the dining room has a custom-made table inspired by one owned by the artists Jackson Pollock and Lee Krasner, and IKEA Parsons-style tables got lacquer-smooth paint jobs.

Best of all, Hughes added personal touches. "I kept thinking, This is the house Carrie built," he recalls, referring to Parker's *Sex and the City* character, Carrie Bradshaw. So he called the show's production designer and asked for an architectural rendering of Carrie's apartment to mount on the sliding panel that hides the built-in television in the master bedroom. "It was a total surprise," Parker says. "At first I thought, Oh, people are going to think I'm an absolute narcissist. But now that the show is over, I'm so glad he did it, because I'm so sentimental about that time." The dining room, however, is her favorite place in the house, hands down. As the actress explains, "When it's filled with people, they become pieces of art that make it even more beautiful." ■

PRECEDING PAGES
Sarah Jessica Parker and Matthew
Broderick's Victorian-style
beach house on Long Island was built in 1865.

OPPOSITE
Inspired in part by the work of 1960s
interior designer Billy Baldwin,
the living room is furnished with a brown denim
sofa, custom-lacquered
IKEA tables, a woven-rattan rocking
chair, and a spatter-print
window seat.

ABOVE
Sarah Jessica Parker and
Matthew Broderick at a charity event in
the Hamptons.

OPPOSITE
In the master bedroom, a
1940s mirrored desk and a portrait of
Parker and Broderick
by Pamela Hanson; the vintage
armchair upholstered
in apple-green Chinese silk was a
flea-market find.

ABOVE LEFT
The guest room features
paneled walls and a pedestal table
painted tulip-red.

ABOVE RIGHT
The beadboard-lined master bath is
a blue-and-white paean
to seaside life; the medicine cabinets, glass
shelves, and sconces
are by Urban Archaeology.

LEFT
The white master bedroom
is accented with pops of color, from
vintage jars to a
Christopher Spitzmiller lamp the
color of a robin's egg.

PIETER ESTERSOHN

Experience good taste early enough in life, and it can become second nature. The photographer Pieter Estersohn got that head start earlier than most, growing up in the San Francisco Bay Area in a house filled with iconic furniture designed by 20th-century greats such as Gio Ponti, Hans Wegner, and T. H. Robsjohn-Gibbings. Still, he admits, "I never really liked California Modern." Instead, he focused his attention on faraway lands. Says Estersohn, "I romanticized the East Coast, all things Egyptian, and English manor houses and castles."

At 15, he spent his spare time repairing antique rugs and used the money that he earned to buy an 1820 English bed. That stately four-poster, now swathed in 1940s wool challis curtains, stands in the master bedroom of the duplex penthouse that he shares with Raul Baez and their son, Elio. Located in a 1903 neoclassical building overlooking historic Gramercy Park, the apartment was dismissed by friends as an irredeemable wreck. Estersohn, however, knew that its interiors (after a little carefully considered renovation) could evoke the feeling of a 1920 Paris atelier, with a bit of an industrial edge and an exotic whiff of Orientalism.

The photographer's theory of interior decoration boils down to a simple mantra: "Some polish. Some patina." The main living space feels both airy and intimate, fresh but touched with history. From the Prouvé daybed to the 19th-century Egyptian cabinet, there's a lot to look at. "I like a monochromatic palette with some punctuation," Estersohn explains. "There's so much going on, but not a lot of colors. That keeps things light and calm." His favorite view looks into the living room from the narrow entrance hall, which is hung with everything from a collage of 19th-century photographs to silkscreens made by Estersohn's mother. A 1950s Hermès frame holds a photo of a personal idol, the intrepid French writer Pierre Loti.

Downstairs is Elio's bedroom. Like any parents, Estersohn and Baez had to figure out a decorative motif that wouldn't look childish in a few years. Furthermore, the space, with windows looking out on a brick wall, needed a real view. So the couple put up a mural made from a blown-up photograph that Estersohn had taken of a state bedroom in a palace in Udaipur. "I just thought Elio would get sick of looking at little lambs when he got older," the photographer says. So it seems certain that another generation with a strong aesthetic sense is already in the making. ∎

PRECEDING PAGES
Photographer Pieter Estersohn, his partner,
Raul Baez, and their son, Elio,
near their home on Manhattan's Gramercy Park.

LEFT
Egyptian mosque lamps dating
from the 17th to the
19th centuries are suspended from the living
area's skylight; the daybed is
vintage Jean Prouvé, the antique inlaid
chairs are Syrian, and the
Tuareg rug is from Marrakech. Carl D'Aquino
collaborated on
the apartment renovation.

ABOVE
The rough-hewn, floor-to-ceiling
bookshelves were inspired by Brancusi's
Endless Column.

INSIDE INFORMATION

■ When you have children, you discover that little sneakers rubbing on silk-velvet upholstery can achieve a remarkably beautiful effect, and that horsehair is a surprisingly great fabric because it's luxurious but cleans up with a sponge.

■ You can't be uptight when kids are learning to feed themselves. Invest in vinyl-covered felt pads for wood dining tables to protect against spills and water marks.

■ Even in a small apartment, children need a designated place where they can get crazy. The wall covering in Elio's room is forgiving; it's so busy, it hides a multitude of sins.

OPPOSITE
The kitchen area features a stainless-steel oven and cooktop by Dacor and an undercounter refrigerator by Sub-Zero; the wall cabinet was designed by Jean Prouvé and Charlotte Perriand, and 1920s French chairs surround a pair of André Arbus tables.

ABOVE
In the hall that leads to the terrace, a collection of vintage frames holds artworks by Estersohn's mother, Betty Estersohn; photographs by Cecil Beaton and Baron de Meyer; and 19th-century odalisques.

TOP RIGHT
The 19th-century frame on the easel was purchased at the Clignancourt flea market in Paris, the painting is Harold Cohen's 12, and the sofa is upholstered in a silk velvet by Larsen; the floors are poured concrete.

RIGHT
The terrace and woven-fabric pergola were designed by Ellen Honigstock.

ABOVE
In the master bedroom, a
vintage Herman Miller bureau and an 1820
English tester bed.

TOP RIGHT
Estersohn installed a 19th-century
Turkish marble cistern for use
as a sink in the master bath; the stained-glass
windowpane is
from a mosque in Tangier.

RIGHT
A graceful metal stair
connects the two floors and adds a sculptural
quality to the downstairs
office; the ceiling fixture is a reissued
Serge Mouille design
and the desk is 1960s Italian.

OPPOSITE
Elio, in his bedroom. The walls are
sheathed in a photo mural
created from a blown-up image Estersohn
took in a palace in Udaipur.

ANH DUONG

*"I've been exposed to so many things,
so many places, so many people. It's a great school of life,
if you're a good student."*

Entering artist Anh Duong's loft and studio in an industrial building in Manhattan's West Village, one gets the sense that time has slowed. Inside it's back to the ragtag 1980s, when loft walls weren't erected by Richard Gluckman or Winka Dubbeldam but by a sculptor friend with a power drill, and kitchens weren't designed in Italy but at the hardware store. It's engagingly bohemian, which is a pretty good description of Duong herself, a Modigliani-style beauty whose half-Spanish, half-Vietnamese features helped make her a muse of couturier Christian Lacroix and a girlfriend of artist Julian Schnabel (she is now married to Barton Quillen, an owner of the Czech-design gallery Prague Kolektiv in Brooklyn) as well as a peerless icon of downtown elegance.

She has used the loft as a studio and, on and off, as an apartment—the place she retreats to for a day, a week, a year—depending on how her fortunes rise and fall. "It's very important to have a space of your own," Duong says. "So even when I am not here full-time, I like to have it as though I could." To that end, there's a proper bedroom, with a magnificent bronze sleigh bed designed by Schnabel and a kitchen big enough to cook for a crowd.

But as the artist, cup of tea in hand, explains the room's history and its contents, it's clear that the assemblage of art, books, and objects have turned the loft into a life-size scrapbook of her nearly 20 years in New York. The off-hand, thrown-together charm is not by happenstance. "I'm a very visual person, and it's important, obviously, that things please my eye," Duong says. Even so, the walls aren't hung with costly and grand works of art—except for the Francis Picabia in the bedroom. Instead, almost every creative treasure has been made by Duong (such as portraits of tastemaker Daniel Romualdez in black tie and the model Karen Elson in nothing at all) or for her by friends like Schnabel, McDermott & McGough, and the late photographer David Seidner. And then there are her many self-portraits, examinations that cast the lissome artist in somewhat stark terms.

"They're not very flattering, no," the artist laughs. "When I am painting someone, I always say, 'I won't make you look beautiful, but it will be a beautiful painting.'" It's enough to make one think that the more glamorous Duong is just an illusion, if it weren't for two dresses—one from Lanvin, another from Lacroix—that hang on a nearby rack. "I like beauty in all forms," she says. "And I've been exposed to so many things, so many places, so many people. It's a great school of life, if you're a good student." ■

PRECEDING PAGES
Model-turned-artist Anh Duong
in the studio of her loft
in Manhattan's West Village.

TOP LEFT
Artworks by Ross Bleckner,
Pablo Picasso,
Julian Schnabel, Damien Loeb,
and others in
Duong's living room.

ABOVE
Self-portraits, including a
diptych, are
displayed with a pair of Louis XV
gilt-wood chairs.

LEFT
In the living room, a 2000
silhouette of Duong, a
still-life photograph by McDermott &
McGough, and an
Egyptian painted-wood mask.

OPPOSITE
A Christian Liaigre cocktail
table is flanked by a
Liaigre sofa and a pair of 1930s French
leather armchairs; Duong
bought the 19th-century gilt-wood
mirror in Paris.

OPPOSITE
In her office/dressing room, Collins works at a Louis XV–style
desk that once belonged to Playboy founder Hugh Hefner. The desk chair is an Austrian Biedermeier
design, with a seat upholstered in vintage leopard
skin. A gallery of portraits of Collins by Karl Lagerfeld, Victor Skrebneski, Gene Meyer,
and others is displayed on the wall.

ABOVE
In the master bedroom, the hand-painted walls
resemble inlaid shagreen. The folding screen is by Marcel Vertès, and the cabinet, which is faced
with panels of woven cane, was designed
by Jean-Michel Frank and owned by the photographer Horst P. Horst.

ACKNOWLEDGMENTS

So Chic wouldn't be half as chic without the efforts of the enormously talented ELLE DECOR team. Our style-savvy art director, Florentino Pamintuan, crafted its rich layouts; designer Meredith McBride added creative input and seemingly boundless energy; photo coordinator Tara Germinsky meticulously organized images called in from around the world; Jay Jennings and Amy Har-Even copyedited the text with great care and diligence; and the unparalleled knowledge and expertise of our erudite executive editor, Mitchell Owens, was truly invaluable. Assistant managing editor Dara Keithley deserves special recognition for her impressive attention to detail and extraordinary dedication to this project.

I thank Dorothée Walliser, head of Filipacchi Publishing, for urging us to create this book, and Stasie McArthur, production director, for her cheerful, patient assistance in seeing it come to fruition.

The generous, consistent support of Jack Kliger, president and CEO of Hachette Filipacchi Media U.S., and Philippe Guelton, executive vice president/COO, is deeply appreciated. And I'm grateful to Jean-Louis Ginibre, my former editorial director and mentor, for his wisdom and sage advice.

I salute the sublimely chic tastemakers on these pages for opening their doors without hesitation, and I owe endless gratitude to the brilliant writers, photographers, and stylists who documented these inspiring interiors and lifestyles for us. The images by photographers Fernando Bengoechea, Henry Bourne, Pieter Estersohn, Simon Upton, and William Waldron are simply dazzling. And the extra dash of magic in our featured homes was added by special projects editor Carlos Mota and design and decoration editor Anita Sarsidi, our resident stylemaker. Anita truly personifies the title of this book.

Margaret Russell
October 2007